The Gorkhas in the Freedom Struggle of India

K. K. Muktan, a retired bureaucrat turned author, is an Indian Gorkha. His grandfather migrated from Nepal to Assam as far back as 1892 and settled down permanently in Tezpur. While still a student, Mr. Muktan joined the Indian freedom movement in 1942 and became a political sufferer. Graduating from St. Anthony's College, Shillong, he did his M.A. in Economics from Allahabad University in 1956. He joined Assam Civil Service (A.C.S.) in 1960 and then the Meghalaya State Civil Service (M.C. S.) in 1975. He held top ranking posts under the Government of Meghalaya.

On his retirement from service in 1989, he turned back to his old predilection of literary works. Having been closely associated with the activities of socio-economic development throughout his service life, Mr. Muktan is deeply interested in the dynamics of Indian societies and has to his credit, books like—*The Legendary Gorkhas, Planning for Retirement, Ganga to Gandaki* and a number of articles in English and Nepali.

The Gorkhas in the Freedom Struggle of India

K. K. Muktan

CONCEPT PUBLISHING COMPANY PVT. LTD.
NEW DELHI-110059

ISBN-13: 978-93-5125-146-0

First Published 2015

Published and Printed by

Concept Since 1974

Concept Publishing Company Pvt. Ltd.
A/15-16, Commercial Block, Mohan Garden
New Delhi-110059 (India)
T: 25351460, 25351794, *F*: 091-11-25357109
E: publishing@conceptpub.com, W: www.conceptpub.com
Editorial Office: H-13, Bali Nagar, New Delhi-110 015, India.

Cataloging in Publication Data--Courtesy: D.K. Agencies (P) Ltd. <docinfo@dkagencies.com>

Muktan, K. K., author.
The Gorkhas in the freedom struggle of India / K.K. Muktan.
pages cm
Includes bibliographical references (pages) and index.
ISBN 9789351251460

1. Gurkha soldiers--Political activity--India. 2. India--History--Autonomy and independence movements. 3. Assam (India)--Politics and government--20th century. I. Title.

DDC 954.035 23

Epitaph

to

I.N.A. Soldiers

"Future generations of Indians who will be born, not as slaves but as free man, because of your colossal sacrifice, will bless your names and proudly proclaim to the world that your, forebears, fought and suffered reverses in the battles in Manipur, Assam and Burma, but throught temporary failure you paved the way to ultimate success and glory."

I.N.A. War Memorial
at Singapore

Dedication

This book is dedicated to

Shaheed Major Durga Malla

who laid down his life for India's liberation
and twenty-two other young Gorkha Jawans
who sacrificed their lives in the Kargil War of 1999

Preface

More than six decades have elapsed ever since India became free from the foreign yoke and yet the written history of India's freedom movement is far from being complete. Many research works have been carried out, many books and articles have been written by Indian as well as foreign historians and yet many facts and events have remained unrevealed, unspoken and unwritten. The Gorkhas' participation in the Indian National Army (INA) or the Azad Hind Fauz is one of the significant events in the annals of India's Freedom Movement which, unfortunately, has not received due attention of Indian historians or, in other words, their writings have not covered all aspects of the episode. Even the missing of Netaji Subhas Chandra Bose, the hero of the INA, is still a mystery, the more of which is probed, the deeper is the enigma. A host of noted historians have dealt with a wide parameters of the Indian National Army including that of its great leader Subhas Chandra Bose but they have chosen to refrain from dealing with the legendary role played by the Gorkha soldiers who joined the INA and fought against the British army to liberate India.

This book is an attempt at throwing some light on the dark corners of the freedom movement of India in the domain of the Gorkha participation in the Azad Hind Fauz that has not been brought to light adequately by historians till today. I believe, this important and integral part of the Indian National Army which has been left unspoken and unknown, if written, will go a long way to open up a new dimension in the history of freedom movement of India.

On 17 February, 1942 45,000 Indian troops including approximately 20,000 Gorkha soldiers joined the INA under the leadership of Captain Mohan Singh. These 20,000 Gorkhas constituted of those who were captured by Japanese earlier in

Malaya and those who surrendered at Singapore together with 45,000 Indian troops on 16 February, 1942 consequent upon the fall of Singapore a day before. Major Fujiwara, the Chief of Japanese Intelligence handed over the 45,000 Indian troops including 20,000 Gorkhas to Capt. Mohan Singh to form INA. Here a question likely to arise is, whether the Gorkhas joined the INA voluntarily or under compulsion. Most of the Gorkha soldiers who joined the INA were the sons of retired Gorkha soldiers who had settled down in India permanently. These Gorkha line boys were educated and bred in Indian environ. They were drawn from politically advanced places like Bhagsu, Dehradun, Nainital, Nalapani, Delhi, Darjeeling, etc. They loved India as their motherland and were inspired by political leaders. The history had that their fathers or close relatives actively participated in freedom movement of India in the past and were members of some political organizations till that time . Therefore, the background from which the Gorkha soldiers hailed strongly suggests that they, except a few coming from Nepal, must have joined the INA out of their own volition without any pressure from any quarter. Those from Nepal and a few others might have followed other Gorkhas as also the case in respect of Indian soldiers.

As INA soldiers, the Gorkhas played a crucial role with their renowned fighting spirit, grit and valour. Their strong and sturdy physique enabled them to bear very rough climate and helped them move forward through the thick and dark jungles and rugged mountains of Burma. Their versatility in the technique of guerrilla fighting added extra capability to Gorkhas which was much appreciated even by Netaji Subhas Bose himself.

The history has it that the civilian Gorkhas living in India have always joined hands with their local inhabitants in their social and political movements in the past. They have never contested them by forming separate political or social organization of their own nor have they competed against the locals for higher job opportunities or for any trade or business. Petty jobs have always satisfied the Gorkhas and they have never vied with anyone for trade and business. During India's freedom movement in 1930s the Gorkhas living in different parts of India rose to the occasion. They joined freedom struggle, suffered imprisonment, confiscation of properties, banishment from the places of residence, dismissal from services. In 1942 Quit India Movement they were lathi charged, beaten and tortured and imprisoned. In 1946, the Gorkhas of Assam joined hands with the local people and raised their voice against the plan for regrouping Assam; and in 1960, when Assamese language bill was opposed tooth and nail by almost all the non-Assamese speakers of Assam, the Gorkhas alone supported the Assamese language bill.

But unfortunately, despite all these good works done, the Gorkhas are not treated kindly by their local neighbours of Assam and the tribal States in the North-East. They think that the Gorkhas have come to India with their mouths and bellies only to become unwanted burden upon them. The people at large are unaware of what the Gorkhas have done for India and the Gorkhas themselves are responsible for this wrong presumption of theirs, because they have not cared to let the people know what they have done and what are they doing for India. The Gorkhas' contributions to India is great — even greater than that of many communities of India. The Gorkhas have laid down their lives for the freedom of India, they have made supreme sacrifice of life and blood for the sovereignty and integrity of India. Gorkhas' contributions to India's security and safety is monumental which is writ large on the pages of Indian military history with their blood. The Gorkha jawans are alert defending Indo-Chinese borders along the Mac-Mahon Line in the North-East ; they are there in the North-West India resolutely protecting Jammu & Kashmir border along the High Himalayas. They are also guarding India's remotest frontier in the Siachin glacier, the world's highest battle field, where extreme cold, high velocity blizzards and dreadful avalanches have rendered human survival extremely difficult. Nevertheless, India's borders are assuredly safe in the hands of redoubtable Gorkha soldiers.

They have made us proud and enablad us to hold our heads high and to tell our Indian brothers - look here, we have made no less contribution to our Mother India than any other community living in this country.

It is my keenest desire of sharing this message with every individual, that has been the abiding motivation which prompted me to take this venture to write this book. I would deem it amply rewarded if the labour of love that has gone into this work succeeds in achieving this goal.

Shillong **K.K. Muktan**

Contents

1

Introduction

India has been the second home to the Gorkhas ever since the beginning of the nineteenth century. According to an estimate nearly six million people of Nepalese origin are permanently settled in various States of India. The origin of the Gorkha settlement in India can be traced from 1815 when the East India Company started recruiting Gorkha sepoys for Indian army immediately after the Treaty of Segauly in 1815. During the Indo-Nepal War the British, for the first time, realized the valour and fighting spirit of the Nepalese army under the command of Amarsingh Thapa and Vir Balabhadra Singh. The British General, David Ochterlony who commanded the Anglo-Nepal war was so much impressed by the bravery, toughness and skill of the Nepalese that he frankly declared during the war — "The Indian soldiers of the Company would never be able to hold their own against the Nepalese in their mountain fastness". In the Gorkhas the British found the right material for Indian army which they were looking for, in the run up to their colonial expansion. The British went headlong with the recruitment of Gorkhas constituting separate units of Gorkha battalions, strictly officered by Englishmen with a view to keeping their martial quality unadulterated.

The first World War brought enormous pressure upon the British military manpower, requiring immediate expansion of Indian army to meet the situation. The Gorkhas who had already proved their mettle in successive wars in Burma and Afghanistan, were the immediate choice for the reinforcement of Indian army. Chandra Shamsher Jang Bahadur Rana, the Prime Minister of Nepal, came out of his way to contribute to the British army with Gorkha recruits. He sent over 55,000 young Gorkhas to be part of the Indian army and another 18,000 Nepali soldiers to take up garrison duties in India. The exodus of Nepalese young population from Nepal was so massive, it is said, that the agricultural operation of the small Himalayan kingdom almost came to a grinding halt during the period of war.

The Second World War witnessed yet another boost in Gorkha recruitment. Yuddha Shamsher Jang Bahadur Rana, the Prime Minister of Nepal responded to the war efforts magnificently with supply of Gorkha young men in tens of thousands. The Gorkha regiments of Indian army expanded all time high pushing the total strength from twenty battalions to fifty-five, composed of ten Gorkha Regiments.

Considering the ever burgeoning demand for Gorkha recruits the Government of India evolved an idea — it allowed the Gorkha Sepoys to bring their families to India, so that, in the long run, part of the recruits needed could be obtained from their children and the Government would be less dependent on Nepal for future requirement of recruits. This scheme was carried out vigorously. Since 1864, Gorkha Regimental Homes were established all over India wherever Gorkha Rifles were stationed.[1] Gorkha soldiers married in Nepal were liberally granted travel expenses for bringing their families. Schools were established for education of their children, the crop for future recruits to Indian army. Other amenities like hospitals, clubs, dhobis, barbers etc. were also provided. The retired Gorkhas who wanted to settle down in India with their families were allotted lands in the vicinity of the Regimental Centres. The retired Gorkhas were also given employment in civil and military offices as Peons, Choukidars, Darwans and Babarchis for earning their livelyhood. Soon, clusters of Gorkha community settlement grew up around the Regimental Centres with schools, temples, shops, bazaars and other infrastructural amenities. This is what may be called the genesis of the Nepalese diaspora into India.

Side by side with the recruitment to Indian army, large number of Gorkha young boys were also enlisted in other para-military forces like Cachar Levy, Assam Rifles, State Police Constabularies etc. ever since 1835, the year of raising Cachar Levy in Assam. The Gorkha boys with their loyalty, hardihood and courage were preferred to the local tribes like Assamese, Manipuris, Kukis and they were liberally recruited in all the semi-military organizations. From 1870, onwards the Gorkhas began to dominate the rolls in all Frontier Police of Assam, pushing up their percentage to fifty of the total strength.[2] By the close of the nineteenth century the Gorkha army Headquartes like Dehradoon, Dharamsala, Darjeeling, Shillong, Kohima, Manipur, Aijawl, were already the places of Nepali concentration.

Towards the close of the nineteenth century AD, a third stream of civilian immigrants, utterly bereft of socio-economic justice under the autocratic Rana rule, started migrating into India particularly towards the North Eastern India. These Nepali migrants settled down in Assam and took to farming and cattle rearing. In Assam land was plenty and grazing reserves for cattle rearing were opened by the Government on payment of grazing fee along the northern bank of Brahmaputra *char*-land or *chavari* (dereliction of river). The local tribal and Assamese people were slothful, self-content and unwilling to do hard work while the Government was acutely starving for revenue which was needed to meet the cost of military establishment required for the consolidation of British rule in the North-East Frontiers and 'civilizing the hill tribes'[3] who often committed forays of head-hunting. Government wanted to bring more land under tillage for augmenting land revenue. Waste lands covered with thick jungles were surveyed, land revenue assessed and settlements were given liberally to Nepali immigrants. Major H. Vetch, Deputy Commissioner, Darrang wrote to J.M. Mills — "In a country so abounding with waste land as Assam and with so scanty a population, Government may well part with a portion on any terms if thereby settlers be induced to come into the country." Hard working and enterprising Nepali farmers who had never owned a shred of land in Nepal had the best of their times to come down from Nepal and grab free land in Assam. They occupied waste land to their choice and working capacity, cleared the jungle and cultivated all varieties of crops locally grown there. The land area possessed by Nepali immigrants increased swiftly from 17,000 acres in1913-14 to 28,000 acres in 1919-20.[4] In Darrang, Lakhimpur and Sibsagar districts sugarcane cultivation was the main crop grown by the Nepalis and large areas were brought under this cultivation. Even today some places in those areas are named as Kuiherbari (Kuiher= sugarcane, bari=cultivated field). The flow of Nepalese immigrants continued and their population increased from 38,306 in 1931 to 3,49116 in 1971, according to Assam census reports. Simultaneously, in 1939-40 the total land occupied and cultivated by Nepalese rose to 1,04,773 acres.[5]

Rearing of cattle and production of milk were monopoly of the Nepalis who kept large *Bathans* (cattle farms) in Nagaland, Manipur, Khasi and Jaintia Hills, Garo Hills and almost all the districts of Assam. The official record of cattle farming business by the Nepalis in Assam goes back to 1892 when the number of tax paying bufloes was registered at 13,025 and the number of cows 462 for which grazing tax amounting to Rs. 6,772 was paid.

The Indian Nepalis, who have been living in India since the last couple of centuries, have adopted India as their home-land and followed the culture and language of their neighbours with a sense of close affiliation, no matter wherever they live and with whichever Indian community they come into contact. They have socially and politically integrated themselves and joined hands with the sons of the soil for every socio-political cause including the freedom movement of India and suffered imprisonments as well as martyrdom. They have identified themselves with their Indian neighbours in their daily socio-cultural intercourse; they speak local languages and dress themselves like their local counterparts of the hills and the plains wherever they live. To quote Prof. A.C. Sinha, "Most of these residents (Gorkhas) have adapted themselves to the local situation in such a way that they are counted among the indigenous people with all the benefits even though they have their own communities and their own way of life, speak their language, maintain their own traditions. But the Nepalis have a great capacity to assimilate themselves with the hill communities. They adopt the language of their neighbourhood, contract marital alliances, and turn out to be an inseparable part of the local economy"[6]. This is especially true about the Gorkhas living in the North-Eastern States where the ethno-political consciousness among the local communities is menacingly high.

They assimilated themselves not only socially and culturally but also politically co-operated with the local inhabitants as and when occasion arose. During the time of freedom movement they did not lag behind in contributing their mights in the task of getting freedom for India. In the wake of Mahatma Gandhi's non-co-operation movement during 1920s when the people of India, irrespective of caste, creed and religion, joined hands together under the leadership of Mahatma Gandhi, the Gorkhas too rose to the occasion. Initially the elite section of the Gorkhas from

Darjeeling, Calcutta, Banaras and Dehradun spearheaded the cause of nationalist movement through separate social and political organizations. Side by side with the activities of these socio-political organizations the press also played its own role to educate people by publication of various news magazines and periodicals in Nepali language. The Nepali periodicals, besides writing on social and cultural aspects, published articles on Mahatma Gandhi's doctrine of non-violence and non-co-operation and *Swadeshi* movement and instilled feeling of nationalism among the Gorkhas. The British government was, however, extremely careful to see that the seed of nationalism did not grow among the Indian Gorkhas, who produced the Gorkha recruits for Indian army. British wanted that the Gorkha young boys should not be adulterated by political ideologies which might erode their loyalty to the Crown and, therefore, they kept strict vigilance on them. One Nepali periodical named *Gorkhali* was proscribed by Government of India in 1922 under Indian Vernacular Press Act 1910 on the suspicion that it disseminated nationalist ideas among the Gorkhas. Another Nepali news magazine was ordered to deposit security for maintenance of good behaviour under the same Press Act, as a result of which it ceased to publish at all. Strict confidential instructions were issued by the Government of India, from time to time, to all Deputy Commissioners and Superintendents of Police to keep close watch on the political activities of Indian Gorkhas and to prevent them from indulging in politics

The echoes of Mahatma Gandhi's clarion call for non-co-operation movement, found their ways into the hills and plains of India. In Darjeeling a good number of Gorkhas joined the Indian National Congress and took active part in *Satyagraha* movement under the guidance of Nepali leaders like Dal Bahadur Giri, Jonbir Sapkota and Prithiman Lama. Mahatma Gandhi's visit to Darjeeling in 1921 brought about a new enthusiasm among the Gorkhas who met him personally and became influenced by him. (S.K. Singh, Tribal Movement in India, p. 342). A political leader Bhagat Bir Tamang was arrested and severely beaten by police for his active participation in the non-co-operation movement and put in prison where he died in 1923. He was the first political martyr among the Nepalis in India.

In Calcutta, the hub of the Revolutionary group of national

activists, Gorkha youths coming from various parts of India and Nepal for study were inspired by the firebrand leaders like Aurobindo Ghose, Bhupendranath Dutta, Rash Behari Bose, Prafulla Chaki, etc., who wanted to wrest freedom from the hands of the British by violent means. For this purpose a group of Gorkhas under the leadership of Khadak Bahadur Bist, a law student of Calcutta University and General Secretary of Calcutta Gorkha League, had established secret nexus with army cantonment to enlist support of Gorkha soldiers. Khadak Bahadur Bist was arrested in May 1930 for attempting to loot the Government salt depot at Dharsana together with 13 others, 150 miles from Bombay and was imprisoned at Sabarmati jail with his thirteen Gorkha associates.

The Gorkhas who had been living for generations in the hills and plains of Assam (North-East) responded magnificently to the call given by Mahatma Gandhi and joined hands together with other local Indians. They joined the National Congress under the leadership of Babu Chhabilal Upadhyaya, and Assamese leaders like Tarunram Phukan, Nabin Chandra Bardoloi, Dr. Hem Chandra Baruah, Amiya Kumar Das, Kuladhar Chaliha, Gopinath Bordoloi, etc. The Gorkhas actively took part in the non-cooperation movement of 1921 protesting against the repressive measures taken by government and the heinous killing of innocent people at Jalianwalla Bag on 13 April, 1919. They boycotted foreign clothes and used home woven clothes. They helped collection of Tilak Swaraj Fund and boycott government offices, schools and colleges. Babu Chhabilal Upadhyaya took the leadership of the Nepali community of Assam during non-co-operation movement of Mahatma Gandhi in 1921. He was arrested and imprisoned in Tezpur jail for six months for taking part in non-co-operation movement. His younger brother, Hari Prasad Upadhyaya was also imprisoned for the same offence for three months.

Dalbir Singh Lohar was another Gorkha leader from Dibrugarh, Assam who started his political career as Congress volunteer as early as when he was a school student. In 1930 he suffered imprisonment for three months for joining the agitation against the Cunninghum Circular, a political issue raised by the National Congress. During the period of Civil Disobedience movement in 1930 he was arrested for the second time and was detained in Dibrugarh jail for two months.

Bhakta Bahadur Pradhan of Dibrugarh joined Congress in 1934. He was an active leader of the Assam Oil Company Labour Union. He lost his service as Motor Mechanic and Fitter in the Assam Oil Company for his involvement in the Labour Union strike. In December 1940, Bhakta Bahadur Pradhan was externed from Assam by an order of the Governor of Assam.

During Quit India movement of 1942 the Gorkhas of Assam took part in the movement in large number. They held mass meetings, resorted to hartals and processions. The public meetings, and processions were forcibly dispersed by the police and the people were lathi charged. The Gorkhas organized demonstrations defying the restriction as a result of which they suffered imprisonment in different jails of Assam. Among those who were imprisoned were, Babu Chhabilal Upadhyaya, Dalbir Singh Lohar, Bhakta Bahadur Pradhan, Ramlal Upadhyaya, Bishnulal Upadhyaya, Jainarayan Upadhyaya, Kashinath Luitel, Homnath Guragain, etc.

Dehradun, the hive of enlightened Gorkha ex-servicemen, was quick to be involved into the freedom movement of India from its very early stage . From the beginning of the twentieth century the Gorkhas of Dehradun evinced keen interest in the Arya Samaj movement led by Swami Dayananda Saraswati whose doctrine of *Swaraja, Swabhasa and Swadharma* attracted the Gorkhas. Madan Singh Gorkha was the first person among the Nepalis to spearhead the cause of Arya Samaj movement who played a leading role as the Secretary and later as President of Dehradun Arya Samaj from 1902 to 1907. Through this organization they came under the influence of great National leaders like Lala Lajpat Rai who sowed the seed of socio-religious and political awareness among the Gorkhas of Dehradun. Gopal Singh Thapa a retired personnel of the Survey of India and a dedicated social worker of Dehradun, sacrificed everything of his life for the freedom of India. He was imprisoned several times and his pension on which his family depended was confiscated by the British Government. Another staunch Congress worker Dhruba Singn Thapa suffered severe police atrocities, got his house and property confiscated, lost his wife while in prison and after his release from jail, he spent the rest of his life in abject poverty sharing a room in the Congress office.

In 1930s, when the Civil Disobedience movement launched by Mahatma Gandhi swept the country the Gorkhas of Dehradun, Nalapani and Delhi rose to the occasion and rallied under the banner of the Indian National Congress. Gorkha leaders like Dhruba Singh Thapa, Riths Singh, Hukum Singh, Dal Bahadur Thapa, Lalbir Newar, etc., together with other Gorkha men, women and children held picketing, demonstrations and courted arrest.

****

The Gorkha soldiers also joined in the freedom movement of India by changing sides for INA and fighting back against the British Government. The Gorkha's participation in the INA or the Azad Hind Fauz is one of the significant annals in the history of India's freedom movement which, unfortunately, has not received due attention of India's historians. A host of noted historians have written exhaustively on the Indian National army including about its great leader Subhas Chandra Bose but they have very conveniently chosen to refrain from dealing with the legendary role played by the Gorkha soldiers who joined the INA and fought against the British army to liberate India. Many movies and electronic visuals have also projected on the role played by the Indian soldiers in the Azad Hind Fouz but very little or nothing at all has been highlighted about the Gorkhas who made supreme sacrifices by their lives for the sake of the country's freedom. Some writers like Field Marshall William Slim (*Defeated into Victory*,1956) and Arthur Campbell (*The Siez: A Story From Kohima*,1956) have given a volume of information about the Second World War in Burma but they have omitted to mention anything about the Gorkhas who changed sides and joined their enemy, the Japanese. Peter Harclerode and David Raynolds (*Gurkhas*, 2003) who have written details about the many reverses suffered by British and Indian Army in the hands of the Japanese troops have mentioned that only twenty-six Gorkhs changed the side while, in reality, not less than twenty thousand Gorkhas had joined the INA. Byron Farwell, a British historian (*The Gurkhas*,1984) has squarely denied any Gorkha having joined the INA except one Gorkha line boy named Durga Singh Lama who is said to have been captured by the British troops and hanged to death. Thus the history has been twisted conveniently to suit their purpose of concealing events detrimental to their interests.

On 15 February, 1942 Singapore fell to the Japanese and the next day the British army laid down their arms and surrendered at Singapore. On 17 February, 45,000 Indian prisoners of war (POW) joined the INA under the leadership of Captain Mohan Singh, an Indian army officer captured earlier by Japanese troops. There were approximately 20,000 Gorkha soldiers among the above 45,000 Indian army who surrendered to Japanese as POWs. Most of these Gorkha POWs were the sons of retired Gorkha soldiers who had settled down permanently at Dehradun, Nainital, Bhaksu, Delhi, Darjeeling, Nalapani, etc. They were educated and bred in Indian environment. They loved India as their motherland and were inspired by nationalistic ideas. For this reason they came forward willingly to join the INA. The inspiring speech of Captain Mohan Singh and Pritam Singh delivered at Ferrar ground on 17 February, 1942 was well received by the Gorkhas who willingly joined the INA.

As INA soldiers, the Gorkhas played a crucial role with their classic fighting spirit, grit and valour. Their physical hardiness and climatic endurance helped them to push forward through the thick jungles and mountain fastness of Burma. Their versatility in the technique of guerrilla fighting added extra capability to Gorkhas which was much appreciated even by Netaji Subhas Chandra Bose.

Most of the Gorkhas were enlisted in the Bahadur Group of the INA which, as a striking force of the INA was responsible to take the lead in the offensives. It was the Bahadur Group which took the leading role in attacking and breaking the British Indian column while advancing towards Imphal and Kohima. It was this Bahadur Group again which suffered the heaviest casualties. Naik Man Bahadur Thapa of the First Bahadur Group was killed in action during the offensive in the Arakan. Havildar Sital Bahadur of the First Bahadur Group was killed in a hand to hand fight against the British force near Ramakori, Burma in August 1944. Captain Sher Bahadur Bhandari who belonged to Durga Malla's 2/1 Gorkha Rifles and joined INA together with him, was seriously injured during the fight near Rangoon and died later in Burma Hospital. He was also in the Bahadur Group. Thus we find in record as many as twenty-five Gorkha soldiers were killed including Durga Malla and Dal Bahadur Thapa who laid down their lives fighting against the British force. (A list of these INA soldiers is given at Appendix-III). These were only a few Gorkha soldiers whose names were recorded by Dr. P.N. Chopra, in his book *Who is Who of Indian Martyrs*, Vol. I, 1969 but there were many more others of the INA Gorkhas who were killed in encounter, maimed and missing whose names are either not known or not recorded. There were also a good number of Gorkha soldiers who acquitted themselves well in the war and received *Azad Hind Fouz* awards and medals for their fighting spirits and show of extra-ordinary bravery and absolute contempt for danger.

The Gorkha soldiers, fighting side by side with the Japanese troops advanced through the thick of battle against the British army and finally set their feet on the Indian soil at Kohima on 6 April,1944. Another column of INA advanced towards Imphal but eventually, before they reached Imphal the Japanese troops had to retreat back due to logistic adversities. The Gorkhas, in their effort to live up to the high ideals of their great leader Netaji, displayed extreme bravery and laid down their lives in hundreds. Two valiant Gorkhas – Major Durga Malla and Captain Dal Bahadur Thapa were captured while on duty by the British troops. They were taken to Delhi jail and after brief trial were hanged to death.

* * * * * * * *

This book has been divided into twelve parts, the first part being introduction. The second part gives us an overview of the Gorkhas living in India. It focuses on the origin of Gorkha settlement in India since 1815 when the British started recruitment of Gorkhas and the settlement of retired Gorkha soldiers in India under the patronage of the British Government. The book also highlights on the large scale migration of civilian Nepalese into India both before and after India's independence and tries to analyse the causes of such immigration. Finally it deals with the prevailing socio-cultural relations between the Gorkhas and the local Indians *vis-à-vis* the ethnic problems faced by the Gorkha community living in the North East India.

Part three deals with the nationalist movement in India, its origin and development. It also gives a brief account of the freedom struggle under the leadership of Mahatma Gadhi at various stages, starting from Satyagraha movement during 1917s, Non-Co-operation movement in 1920s, Civil disobedience movement during 1930s and finally the Quit India Movement in 1942.

Part four of the book discusses about the participation of Gorkhas in the freedom movement of India in different parts of the country where Gorkhas are in concentration — in Darjeeling, Kolkata, Dehradun and in the far North Eastern region. It highlights on the sufferings of the freedom fighters through imprisonment, dismissal from service, physical torture and banishment from the places of residence.

Part five gives a true account of the role played by the Gorkha soldiers in the Indian National Army under the leadership of Netaji Subhas Chandra Bose. It tells about the valour, grit and fighting spirit, of the Gorkha soldiers which they had demonstrated under adverse logistic condition and accounts for the supreme sacrifice made by them for the liberation of India from the yoke of the British.

Part six is the life sketch of Major Durga Malla, INA soldier, who laid down his life at the altar of Mother India for the sake of her freedom from British rule. Martyr Durga Malla was captured by British troops while on duty of espionage in Burma and brought to Delhi jail. He was executed by hanging until death on 25 August, 1944 after a brief trial at the historic Red Fort. Part seven gives an account of the Kargil war of 1999 and the sacrifice of lives given by Gorkha boys.

From Part eight to twelve of the book have been devoted in giving life sketches of five prominent Gorkha freedom fighters – Babu Chhabilal Upadhyaya, Dalbir Singh Lohar, Bhakta Bahadur Pradhan Bishnulal Upadhyaya, and Captain Ram Singh Thakuri.

References

1. Muktan, K.K., *The Legendary Gorkhas*, 2002, Guwahati, p. 212.
2. *Ibid.*, p. 72.
3. Shakespear, Col. L.W., *History of Assam Rifles*,1929.
4. Report on the Land Revenue Administration of Assam, 1919-1920.
5. Report on the Land Revenue Administration of Assam, Valley Division, 1939-40.
6. A.C. Sinha, The Indian North-East Frontier and the Nepalese immigrants, published in *Himalayan Environment and Culture*, edited by N.K. Rustomji, p. 228.

2

The Gorkhas in India

Although no official figure is available, according to an estimate nearly six million people of Nepalese origin are permanently settled in various parts of India, while approximately four million people of Indian origin are residing in Nepal. Demographically speaking, nearly 16.7 per cent of the total population of Nepal is composed of Indians, while 0.57 per cent of the total population of India is constituted by the people of Nepalese origin. Looking in terms of ratio we find that Nepal has one Indian for every six Nepalese, whereas India has one Nepali for every two hundred Indians. These immigrants, with the exception of some floating population, have permanently settled down in each other's adopted countries as citizens by swearing allegiance to the constitutions of respective countries while their children and grand-children have automatically become the citizens by birth.

The movement of population between the two countries has been primarily caused due to geographical proximity, similarity of languages, cultures and religion besides economic reasons. The existing bilateral agreements between India and Nepal also helped them to move freely without passport and visa and to carry on trade, business or services in their respective adopted countries.

It will be pertinent here to discuss, at some length, about the uniformity and close relationship between the two countries. India and Nepal are two ancient countries with common history and ethno-cultural heritage. Besides these, the two neighboring, countries having been separated by 800 km. long boundary have many things in common as well as in contrast. Both the countries are characterized by natural and geographical diversities and multiplicity of races, religions and languages, and marked by similar political vicissitudes. India is the largest democracy in the world with an area bigger than France, Italy and Spain put together. Pitted with this enormous size of India, Nepal compares a tiny mound that accounts for less than one-twentieth fraction of India's total geographical area. Far more remarkable than its geographical vastness are the enigmatic natural features with diverse altitude, rainfall, climate, soil condition, on its top, the map of Nepal in bold dotted lines which looks like an army insignia on the shoulder flap of India.

Within India, despite the bewildering heterogeneity of ethnicity, culture, religion and the geophysical conditions mentioned above, there exists a deep underlying unity which has kept the Indian people together over the ages as one nation. Coming to Nepal, we can see similar diversities in a wide parameters of ethnicity, culture, language and religion, despite the country being small in size. Its antiquity and heritage are as old as the human civilization itself. Archaeological evidences show that Nepal was inhabited by people at least nine thousand years ago. The earliest record about Nepal can be traced from the *Arthashastra of Kautilya* written as far back as third century B.C. The *Skanda Purana* speaks highly of the temples and shrines of Nepal and their sanctity and holiness. Nepal's ancient art and architecture are still visible in the temples, shrines and buildings around Kathmandu, Bhatgoan and Lalitpur which are incredibly glorious.

Like India, Nepal too received settlers of various racial affiliations from the north and the south ever since the dim past and till the advent of fourteenth century A.D. From the north came the people of Tibeto-Burman linguistic group who crossed over the high Himalayas through mountain passes called Kuti, Hatia, Kerong, Mustang etc., while from south, that is India, entered more dominant reces like the Kiratas, Lichchavis, Thakurs, Mallas and Rajputs. These new comers from northern India who were advanced in knowledge, culture and religion, vanquished the ruling chiefs there and founded new kingdoms in Nepal. They bot only ruled over the people of the new found country but also gradually initiated them into their own religion, first into Buddhism and then Hinduism. They brought them, finally under the fold of Hinduism and the elaborate Vedic social system. The proximity to Nepal and its 300 km long open border helped Hindu priests and preachers of India to enter Nepal freely and preach Hinduism and

Indian culture. Nepalese history tells us that during the reign of king Rudradeva (635-656 A.D.) one Sankaracharya, a bigoted Hindu preacher, visited Nepal under whose instigation the king of Nepal persecuted the Buddhist monks, destroyed Buddhist monasteries and burned down Buddhist libraries. Under the royal patronage of the ruling Hindu dynasties, Indian art, culture, religion and architecture continually found their way into the Sub-Himalayan country, which in course of centuries developed into a typical orthodox Hindu kingdom. This is the reason why we can see even today numerous Buddhist stupas and Hindu temples in Nepal. The history of Nepal is, essentially an account of the assimilation of two peoples who lived side by side meeting and mixing up their cultures, traditions and languages for centuries. India and Nepal, thus share a common history and heritage which are so intricately woven up each other that it is difficult to comprehend the one without understanding the other.

Looking from this angle Nepal may be perceived as a miniature India with its wonderful blend of variegated ethno-cultural traits, legends and faiths with those of India. If India is, as stated by Radha Kumud Mookerjee, "a museum of cults and customs creeds and cultures, faith and tongue, racial types and social systems", then Nepal is verily the confluence of them all. Both India and Nepal have inherited from the past common system and forms of art, culture, literature, philosophy, metaphysics, astronomy, astrology and medicine. The people of both the countries have been influenced by the same Vedas, Upanishads and Puranas which have permeated deep down into their socio-religious psyche. The great epics of *Ramayana* and *Mahabharata* are held in the highest esteem in both the countries. Great Prophets like Buddha and Mahavira, and the mighty kings like Ashoka and Vikramaditya belong to Nepal as much as to India. This being the kind of relationship between India and Nepal from the ancient times till today, it is imperative for every citizen of India and Nepal to know the history of one another's country.

The history and origin of the settlement of Gorkhas in India can be traced from early nineteenth century when, immediately after the Treaty of Segauli in 1815, the British started recruitment of Gorkha Sepoys for Indian Army. According to E.A. Gait, colonial historian, the Gorkha soldiers penetrated into Assam as early as

1817, nine years prior to formal annexation of Assam, ostensibly to drive out the marauding Burmese.[1] Many of these Gorkha sepoys when retired from service preferred to remain in India as the British Government provided them with employment in other civil offices as choukidars, chaprashis, peons etc. "A Nepali used to get the benefit of preference over others including the indigenous population for certain jobs".[2] The British encouraged Gorkha population to grow up in India with the view that the children of these Indian Gorkhas could be recruited in Indian Army. With this end in view, the Government established Gorkha Regimental Homes at several Army Headquarters in 1864 to provide accommodation to the families of the Gorkha soldiers and granted travel expenses to Gorkha soldiers married in Nepal to bring their families to live in India.[3] Captain John Bryan Neufvile, the Commanding Officer and Political Agent for Upper Assam had always preferred Gorkhas. He said they were "proverbially brave, active and capable of enduring fatigue both in the hills and jungles and free from the prejudices which the Hindus of the Regular Troops were invariably accustomed". Lands were settled to the ex-service men in the vicinity of the Regimental Homes, where schools and hospitals were established for the Gorkha families. Captain Francis Jenkins, in his report of 1832 "recommended that instead of pensions the ex-soldiers of the local corps should be given grant of land".[4] With the passage of time many other para-military forces like State constabulary, Assam Rifles, Central Reserve Police Force, Border Security Force, etc., were raised in various parts of India in which large number of Gorkhas were recruited. Together with the Gorkha recruits there came from Nepal civilian Nepalese seeking self-employment in rural occupation like agriculture, animal husbandry and manual labour and petty jobs.

Behind this large scale immigration of civil population from Nepal, there were certain strong push factors which constantly pressurized a large number of Nepalese to seek their livelihood outside Nepal. These factors were (1) increasing fragmentation of landholdings, (2) heavy exploitation of landless tenants by the landlords, (3) Indebtedness, (4) ecological crisis through deforestation, (5) rising population and unemployment, (6) poverty and hunger of common people, and (7) oppression of the Rana rulers. Together with these push factors from Nepal there were also certain pull factors from India which propelled the Nepalese migration into India and especially into Assam. These pull factors were (1) the colonial patronage; (2) wide scope for job opportunities in Indian army, paramilitary forces, State constabularies, office peons, choukidars, darwans etc; (3) abundance of land in the hills and plains; and (4) wide scope for cultivation and cattle grazing.

The Nepalis population continued to grow during the postcolonial period too. The Article 7 of the Indo-Nepal Treaty of Peace and Friendship 1950 granted the nationals of one country in the territories of the other the same privileges in the matter of residence, ownership of property, participation in trade and commerce, movement and other privileges of a similar nature. The people of one country could enter into the country of other without any restriction and stay as long as one desired or could carry out any trade or occupation. No passport or visa is required to cross the border. Thus the friendship between the two countries is unique and time honoured which no other two countries in the world possess. This open border policy adopted by India and Nepal is not a recent arrangement ; it had been there ever since the British Rule when the peoples from the two countries had been, as a matter of course, crossing each other's borders freely and settling down in their adopted countries at their will. This practice, over the ages, has eventually resulted in large scale inter-migration and settlement of people in both countries.

The Indian Nepalis, who have settled in India over the last couple of centuries, have adopted India as their home-land and followed the culture and language of their neighbours with a sense of close affiliation, no matter wherever they live and with whichever Indian community they come in contact. They have socially and politically integrated themselves and joined hands with the sons of the soil for every socio-political cause including the freedom movement of India and suffered imprisonments as well as martyrdom. Monirul Hussain writes, The Nepalis of earlier generation had impressive records of fighting for India's independence in Assam. The elite Nepalis of Darjeeling, Calcutta, Banaras and Dehradun spearheaded the cause of nationalist movement by forming their own political organizations like the Hillmen Association of Darjeeling, the Gorkha Association of Calcutta and the All India Gorkha League of Dehradun, etc., Shaheed Bhagat Bir Tamang of Karseong who joined non-co-operation movement and died in Darjeeling jail in 1923 became the first political martyr among the Nepalis. Gopal Singh Thapa of Dehradun sacrificed everything of his life in freedom movement. He was imprisoned several times and his pension was confiscated by the British Government. Major Durga Bahadur Malla of Dehradun joined Indian National Army of Subhas Chandra Bose and fought against the British army while he was captured in Burma and brought to Delhi jail. He was hanged to death by the British after a brief trial in 1944. The Nepalis of Assam rose to the occasion under the able leadership of Chhabilal Upadhyaya, Bhakta Bahadur Pradhan, Dalbir Singh Lohar, Bisnulal Upadhyaya, etc. During 'Quit India' movement they suffered imprisonment several times. Under the inspiring leadership of Subhas Chandra Bose, a large number of Gorkha soldiers imprisoned by the Japanese in Malaya and Singapore (mostly Indian Gorkhas) joined Indian National Army in 1942. They fought grim battles against the British army in the jungles of Burma and laid down their lives for India's freedom. Two of them, viz., Major Durga Singh Thapa and Captain Dal Bahadur Thapa were captured by the British army, brought to Delhi jail and hanged to death after a brief trial at Delhi Red Fort. The contribution of the Gorkha soldiers for India's sovereignty and integrity is monumental which is writ large with their blood on the pages of Indian military history. Today, the Gorkha jawans are defending Indo-Chinese borders along the Mc-Mahon line in the North-East; they are there on the North-West frontiers resolutely protecting Jammu and Kashmir. They are also there in Siachen glacier, the worlds highest battle field, where extreme cold, high velocity blizzards and dreadful avalanches have rendered human survival extremely difficult. India is ever safe in the hands of loyal and redoubtable Gorkhas.

The Nepalis of Assam joined hands with Asamiyas and raised their voices against the Grouping Scheme proposed by the Cabinet Mission of 1946. They also fought for the official recognition of Asamiya language as the medium of instruction up to graduate level at par with English. They have identified themselves with their Indian neighbours in their daily socio-cultural intercourse ; they speak local languages and dress themselves like their local counterparts of the hills and the plains wherever they live. To quote Prof. A.C. Sinha, "Most of these residents (Gorkhas) have adapted themselves to the local situation in such a way that they are counted among the indigenous people with all the benefits even though they have their own communities and their own way of life, speak their language, maintain their own traditions. But the Nepalis have a great capacity to assimilate themselves with the hill communities. They adopt the language of their neighbourhood, contract marital alliances, and turn out to be an inseparable part of the local economy".[5] This is especially true about the Gorkhas living in the North-Eastern States where the ethno-political consciousness among the local communities is menacingly high.

It is, however, tragic to say that despite all these contributions made by them, the Nepalis living in the North-Eastern States are not treated kindly by their Indian neighbours. They are looked upon as unwanted intruders into their homes, as foreigners and are victimized in various ways, threatened, assaulted, killed and, at times, uprooted from their hearths and homes. The political turmoil that rocked Assam during 1979-84 under the aegis of All Assam Students Union (AASU) and Assam Ganasangram Parishad (AGSP) recorded some of the worst ethnic violences in Indian history. As per official report submitted by the Government of Assam to the Centre, the agitation took a toll of 3,059 lives only within the period of six months, from January to June 1983, which includes a large number of Nepalis.[6] Earlier in February, 1983 over 1200 people, mostly women and children were butchered to death at Nellie about 70 Km east of Guwahati in Nagoan district.[7] It may be mentioned here that the Assam Movement and the mayhem started in the middle of 1979 and continued till the Assam Accord was concluded in 1985.

The foreign national issue of Assam found an echo in Manipur with Shri Daben Singh, President, State Students Co-ordination Committee, demanding immediate deletion of names of foreigners from voter lists and then deportation from Manipur.[8] In another incident, about 500 homesteads were set ablaze at Sagolmang, 25 Km from Imphal on the night of 1st May, 1980 rendering homeless over 2500 people, mostly Nepalis. A group of 300 persons armed with firearms and other lethal weapons from nearby areas swooped down on the village and went on committing arson which left 18 cattle and many other domestic animals charred to death.[9] The Revolutionary Communist Party of India (RCPI) in a booklet (7-8 pages) published by the party demanded immediate action to stop the unabated flow of Nepalese nationals into Assam.

The ethnic violence perpetrated by the Khasi Students Union (KSU) against the Gorkhas of Meghalaya in 1987 sent the greatest shock to the Nepalis who lived there for generations in close cultural assimilation and friendship. Many of them were indiscriminately assaulted and killed, their dwelling houses, cattle sheds and school buildings were set on fire and forced them to flee their homes for Nepal. Approximately 12000 *Khutiwala* Nepalis (cattle rearers) fled away leaving behind their cattle or selling them at throw-away prices. According to an official source more than 6,600 persons took shelter in the government run Relief Camps for more than four months.[10]

What is most deplorable is that, the Assam Gorkha Sammelan the only representative body of the Nepalis living in North-East has been urging upon both India and Nepalese governments to stop free crossing of border from both sides so that the Indian Nepalis, who are already settled in India are not suspected to be Nepalese nationals. In this connection the following predicaments of the Nepalis of the North-East as asserted by Dr. T.B. Subba, Professor Anthropology Department, North Eastern Hill University, deserves mention here.[11]

"One, the foremost predicament (of the Nepalis) is the fear of eviction. This fear is based on past experience of the Nepalis from States like Manipur, Mizoram, Nagaland, Assam and Meghalaya."

"Two, one of the main reasons why they fear eviction is their political status in the region as foreigner. Most of them are bona fide citizens of the country with voting rights and with ownership of immovable properties. But politically they are categorised as foreigners and treated at par with the immigrants from Bangladesh."

"Three, on account of the open border between Nepal and India even the descendants of those Nepalis who got settled in India in early nineteenth century and are of Indian origin may be suspected to have come from Nepal."

"Four, the Nepalis in the region have been experiencing a loss of their identity."

There is, thus, an urgent need, on the part of the Nepalese Government, to remove these long standing predicaments of the Indian Nepalese through negotiations and bilateral agreements with the Government of India. As the time passes and the tribal people competing for wider field of resources in the region there is possibility of their becoming more hostile to the Nepalis living there. Therefore, the only way to contain this situation is to control further influx of Nepalese nationals into the North-East through introduction of Inner Line Permit system which is the current demand of the NGOs as well as the governments of these regions.

Nepali or Gorkha

To an Indian the two terms 'Nepali' and 'Gorkha' are confusing and difficult to make out who is a Nepali or who is a Gorkha. In Indian context both the terms are inter-exchangeable and are applied to mean one and the same person. It is a matter of choice only. In this book I have used these two terms indiscriminately according to the context. But in Nepal the term 'Gorkha, is used in restricted meaning while the term 'Nepali' connotes the people of the country. In other words 'Gorkha' may be said to indicate the nation or country while 'Nepali' stands for the nationality. The term Gorkha is used on more official and specific purposes than Nepali, such as 'Gorkha Raj', 'Gorkha Patra', 'Gorkha Muluk', 'Gorkha Palton', etc. To understand the meaning of the term 'Gorkha' more clearly, we have to go to the root from where the word was coined. The word Gorkha has emerged from the root "Go-ra-kh", the abbreviation of Gorakhnath, the Patron Saint of the principality called Gorkha, that was located in the 'Choubisi' region west of Kathmandu. Prithvi Narayan Shah, the King of Gorkha who is credited to have unified present Nepal in the eighteenth century, was from this Gorkha Principality. He was known as the Gorkha King and his army which conquered the whole of Nepal was known as Gorkha Palton. It was the same Gorkhali force which fought against the British in the Anglo-Nepal War of 1814-16 under the leadership of General Amarsingh Thapa and earned the praise of the British. These Gorkhas were recruited in the Indian army by the British since 1815 and ever since then till today the Gorkhas are continuing in the Indian army. The contemporary Indian Gorkhas living in different parts of India are mostly the descendants of the Gorkha soldiers who settled down permanently in India after their retirement. This is the reason why the Indian Nepalis like to be called themselves as Gorkhas.

Suhas Ghising, the supremo of the Gorkha National Liberation Front (GNLF) is of the opinion that 'Gorkha' should replace the word 'Nepali'. He even asked all Nepalis to leave Darjeeling. (T.B.Subba, 2003, p. 200). The word 'Nepali', according to him, meant a Nepali national and hence should go to Nepal. Ever since that time the controversy whether Indian Nepalis should be called Nepalis or Gorkhas or Gorkhalis has persisted among the Indian Nepalis till today without a broad consensus. Some writers have suggested other terms, like 'Bharpali (Bhartiya Nepali),' Bhargoli'(Bhartiya Gorkhali), Nepamul (Nepali root), etc. This situation has been described as identity crisis by Social Scientists like A.C. Sinha, T.B. Subba, etc. Here the effort is to find out an alternative nomenclature which will give the Indian Nepalis a distinctive identity separate from that of Nepalese nationals so that the Indian people in general and the people of the North-East , in particular, would not mistake them to be the Nepalese nationals. The alternative names suggested above, like 'Bharpali', 'Bhargoli' or 'Nepamul', etc. are not names but sobriquets and, hence, they would not serve the purpose. In this context the effort of Ramkrishna Sharma, Ex-Judge of Calcutta High Court and Subhas Ghising, Chief of GNLF and many others to use the nomenclature of Gorkha in lieu of Nepali is understandable and sounds viable and acceptable alternative to Nepali. It also looks justified for us to make sublime the name of our redoubtable fore-fathers who served in the Indian army and gave their lives for India's safety and sovereignty, by assuming their proud name 'Gorkha' for our identity. The word Gorkha is not a new one in India, as it has already come to be used among the Indian Nepalis since long time. We have/had names like All India Gorkha League, Dehradun (since 1921), Gorkha Sathi, Calcutta (1911), Gorkha Association, Calcutta (1926), Gorkhali, Banaras (1914), Tarun Gorkha, Dehradun (1927), Assam Gorkha Sammelan (1965), Akhil Bhartiya Gorkha Parisangh, Assam Gorkha Students Union etc. Some quarters appear to have their objection about the word 'Gorkha' on the ground that it symbolizes the lowly profession of 'security men or other domestic servants' taken up by many Gorkhas in Indian metropolices. This argument would, however, be synonymous with pointing at the black spots on the bright moon. For the bright name that the Gorkha soldiers have earned for themselves will never be obliterated by a few low status professionals. People of many communities in India are serving in lowly professions. The scavengers, mochis, bhangis are no better than security men, darwans, hotel boys and cooks. There is no reason to shy away from these professions.

This book tells the unvarnished stories about the legendary Gorkha soldiers changing their sides and fighting against the British for India's freedom. It also speaks about the Gorkha civilian freedom fighters who, by their supreme sacrifices, made us proud and enabled us to hold our heads high and tell our Indian counterpart that we have made no less contributions to India than any other community in India.

References

1. M. Hussain, *The Assam Movement*, 1997, Nanak Publication, Delhi, p. 255.
2. *Ibid*, p.260.
3. K.K. Muktan, *The Legendary Gorkhas*, 2002, Spectrum Publishers, Gawahati.
4. Monirul Hussain, *Assam Movement*,1993, Nanak Publications, Delhi.
5. A.C. Sinha, The Indian North East Frontier and Nepali Immigrants, in *Himalayan Environment and Culture* edited by N.K. Rustomji and Charles Ramble, New Delhi, 1990, pp. 217-236.
6. B.L Upadhyaya, *Assame Nepaliharu* (in Nepali), Tezpur, 1984, p.56.
7. *Ibid*, Manirul Hussain, p.141.
8. *Amrit Bazar Patrika*, dated 1st April, 1980.
9. *Assam Tribune*, dated 1st May, 1980.
10. *Shillong Times*, dated 10th, 13th, 14th,17th, and 18th July, 1987.
11. Sinha A.C. and Subba T.B. (Edt). *The Nepalis in The North-East India*, 2003, pp. 205-206.

3

Nationalist Movement and Freedom Struggle of India

The wind of nationalism that swept the whole of Europe and South America during the close of the eighteenth century reached the shore of India after a century. The American War of Independence of 1776 and the French Revolution of 1789 left an impact on the leaders of India. They studied about the American independence war, the national liberation movement of Greece, Italy and Ireland and were deeply impressed by the campaign lodged by their leaders like George Washington, Joseph Mazzini and Garibaldi. They pondered about the despotic rule and domination of the British over India, and wanted to liberate India from foreign yoke. The course of history of the countries around the world and the knowledge of war against foreign domination aroused nationalism and patriotic feeling among the elite section of the Indians. Bal Gangadhar Tilak demanded— "Freedom is our birth right". Prof. Iswari Prasad wrote — "The consciousness of the French that their troubles were due to the Bourbons, led to French revolution; of the British that their troubles were due to the unrestrained prerogatives of the Crown, led to civil war; and of the Indians, that their troubles were due to British rule, led to formation of Indian National Congress".

The British historians maintain that the Indian nationalism is the creation of the British. According to them there was no nationalism in India before the advent of the British, as India was never a nation. It was a land of many people speaking diverse languages, following different faiths, religions and cultures and having no political solidarity among them. They say that the Indians developed the concept of nationalism only during the British rule.

The Indian scholars have, however, refuted this contention.

They have argued that, India, of course, is a country of many *languages cultures and faiths* but in the midst of all diversities there is an underlying unity. No matter, however, politically divided they seem be, they are cast in a wider mould of Vedic culture, common religion, heritage and a shared history. They inherit the same set of Vedas, are inspired by the same sages and prophets and influenced by the same epics — the *Ramayana* and *Mahabharata*. They cherish a common feeling that they belong to one nation and one country ever since the ancient country of Ashoka, to the empire of Akbar, the Mugal emperor which lasted till the advent of the British.

After the British took over from the Mughals, the Indian nationalism grew up partly as an offshoot of modernization initiated by the British and partly as the inevitable repercussion to the British imperial policies of political domination, social repression and economic exploitation. The principal factors leading to the growth and development of Indian nationalism may be summarized as follows.

The social and religious movements of the nineteenth century like the Brahmo Samaj, the Arya Samaj, the Ramkrishna Mission and the Theosophical Society in their own respective ways perceived the glory of ancient India. They generated faith in Indian culture and religion and tried to strengthen it by removing their evil aspects. They also indirectly helped in awakening Indian nationalism and developing unification of Indian people. For, the leaders of these movements were not only social and religious reformers but also true patriots. Raja Ram Mohan Roy, Swami Vivekananda, Swami Dayananda Saraswati, Mrs. Annie Besant were all patriots who tried to reform and revive the rich cultural heritage of ancient India. Through glorification of Indian culture they developed the sense of Indian solidarity and indirectly fostered insurgence of Indian nationalism. Dayananda Saraswati, the founder of Arya Samaj established many schools and Gurukulas and through them infused feeling of patriotism among the children. He was the first person to advocate the concept of *Swadesha-Swaraja-Swabhasa* which went a long way in arousing the feeling of love for own country and its freedom. Swami Vivekananda, the founder of Ramakrishna Mission, too played the role in helping build up Indian nationalism by inculcating a sense of confidence, self glorification and patriotism among the Hindus. Mrs. Annie Besant, the President of the Theosophical Society, helped not only in strengthening Indian nationalism but also putting the political movement of India on an even keel. Thus we can say that the social and religious movements of the nineteenth century contributed a great deal in awakening Indian nationalism.

The introduction of English language also went a long way in the growth of nationalism among the Indian people. The English as a medium of instruction of education facilitated Indians to know the language and to contact with western ideas, culture and institutions. The ideas of Nationalism, democracy, liberty, equality, etc., could infiltrate into India through the books written by men like Rousseu, Burke, James Mill, Herbert Spencer, etc., from which the educated Indians came to know how the Indians were politically suppressed by the British. Many educated Indians went abroad and had the opportunity to come in direct contact with western thoughts and attitudes. That imbued in them the spirit of nationalism, democracy, liberty, freedom, etc. To say the truth, it was the English educated Indians who were primarily responsible for creating political awakening and arousing national consciousness among the Indians which helped in heralding political movements in India. English language being the *lingua franca of the world,* it played a unifying role and broadening of knowledge around the globe. Poet Ravindranath Tagore said, "The Indians knew England through her glorious literature and not through her misdeeds overseas".

The British system of administration and education policy gave rise to a new class of society in India which may be called the middle class of people that consisted of modern educated intelligentsia group. Although this class of people represented a very microscopic minority of India's vast population, it was this middle class that pioneered the nationalist movement of India at its inception. Many scholars, both Indian and European have accepted that the Indian national movement was the brainchild of the educated Indian middle class. P. Spear writes , "The new middle class was a well-integrated all India class with varied background but a common foreground of knowledge, ideas and values — it was a minority of Indian society but a dynamic minority. It had a sense of unity of purpose and hope". The intelligentsia who assimilated the ideas of nationalism and democracy were the first to feel the democratic and national impulse. But subsequently, other classes of people including the peasantry participated and strengthened the national movement.

The establishment of printing press helped circulation of ideas among people through newspapers, books and magazines. A large number of journals and newspapers were published in many regional languages throughout India which carried news of British policy of exploitation and imperial expansion ; their racial arrogance and misbehaviour. In 1877, there were about 169 news papers in India published in vernacular languages and their circulation reached the neighbourhood of one lakh. To mention a few of them — *The Indian Mirror, The Amrit Bazar Patrika, Bombay Chronicle, The Hindu, Patriot, The Mahratta, Kesari,* etc., are some of the pioneering newspapers of the early nineteenth century which took leading part in moulding public opinion in favour of Indian nationalism. This apart, literary works like novels, stories and poems also found their ways into Indian societies from great patriots, writers and poets like Bankim Chandra, Ravindranath Tagore, Bharatendu Harish Chandra, etc., whose pen inspired true love for mother India and awakened strong political consciousness. The beautiful song composed by Bankim Chandra for his novel *Ananda Math, viz., Vande Mataram* has been adopted by Government of India as her national song. The great poem — *Jana, gana, mana* — composed by Ravindranath Tagore is today India's National Anthem. Thus the Indian printing press played a major role in awakening mass national sentiment in India that paved the way for political movement.

The British came to India as a trader and hence the policies adopted by them were always oriented towards financial gain. They wanted to make India a ready market for British manufactured goods and a source of supply of raw materials needed by the factories in England through the adoption of free trade policy which proved suicidal for the Indian small industries. The British drained off the natural resources of India in a most systematic way. Dadabhai Naoroji was the first Indian to point out the extent of economic exploitation done by the British. The deliberate policy of the British to rule over India for their economic benefit, the oppression of rayats, the deprivation of eligible Indians of higher government services and exploitation of India's natural wealth like timber, oil, minerals, etc., wounded the feeling of the Indians. The impact of British rule on Indian economy was disastrous. In 1879 when Lord Lytton abolished import duties on cotton the condition of the Indian cultivators grew from bad to worse. Serious agrarian disturbances took place in Bengal in 1872-73 when heavy burden was imposed on the peasant with enhanced land revenue. Occurrence of famines became a regular feature of Indian economy. During the second half of the nineteenth century as many as 24 famines visited various parts of India which took a great toll of human lives. The oppression of the European indigo and tea planters on the labourers created a strong hatred against the British among general public. The Tariff and Cotton Duties Act 1804 and 1896 brought wide discontentment among the cotton growers. These Acts, obviously designed to serve the interest of British manufacturers, were a severe blow to the cotton industry. Thus, the economic policies of India in all fields — agriculture, heavy industries, finance, tariffs, foreign capital investment, foreign trade, banking etc. — went against the interest of India, as these were all geared to the preservation of colonial economy.

The British made the legislation their handy instrument to suppress the rights and privileges of the Indian people. A number of legislations were enacted by the Government of India during their reign to suit their interest disregard to the rights and interests of the Indians. The Vernacular Press Act 1910 passed during the time of Lord Lytton suppressed the liberty of Indian people to publish newspapers and express the opinion of people. Under this Act anybody found publishing seditious materials, incriminating articles which might go against the government were made punishable. The rigours of this Act was so great that within a period of ten years of the enactment of this law more than 300 newspapers, 350 printing presses and 400 publications were penalized. By introducing Subsidiary Alliance, Lord Wellesley brought many native States under the control of the British regarding foreign affairs. The States had to surrender their external relations to the Company and were to conduct negotiations with other States only through the Company. Taking the plea of providing military aids to the native States the British government interfered with the powers of external affairs of many native princes, like the Nizam of Hyderabad, Nabab of Oudh, the Raja of Tanjore, etc. Thus, while the Subsidiary Alliance proved beneficial to the English it had a demoralizing effect on the Indian princes and proved harmful to the people. Through the introduction of Indian Forest Act 1868 the Government reserved tribal forest for earning revenue and hurt the tribal sentiment by infringement of their right to use forest produce. The Local Self Government Act introduced by Lord Curzon seriously injured the feelings of the Indian people. By the

Indian Arms Act 1878 the Government restricted rights of the people to the use of arms and ammunitions without license. All these antiIndian Acts and legislations of the British aroused great resentment among the Indians which contributed to accelerate the growth of Indian nationalism.

The British policy of introducing rigorous land tenure system and imposing heavy land revenue was greatly resented by cultivators from time to time. The peasant uprising that occurred in different parts of India was another cause of awakening national feeling among the people at the grass root level. The harassment of the zamindars and exploitation of the money lenders were the other potential factors which paved the way for national uprising against the Government. We have seen peasant uprising among the Santhals of Bihar and Orissa in 1854 and 1855. There was also peasant rebellion in 1860 among the indigo cultivators of Bengal. This uprising was directed against the repressive policy of the European indigo planters who were supported by the British government. Again in 1870, an agrarian agitation broke out in East Bengal against the oppressive acts of the zamindars. In Assam, the peasants raised the banner of revolt against imposition of excessive land revenue in 1893-94. The peasant uprisings occurring in various parts of the country are the clear indication of the growing consciousness among the Indian peasants about the policies of exploitation and repression of the British.

On the top of all these facts, what exasperated the Indian leaders most was the attitude of pride and arrogance of the British. They considered themselves as a superior race and looked down upon the Indians as their slaves. They exhibited haughtiness in dealing with Indians and behaved abusively even the Indian women. The British Government disbanded appointment of Indians in high civil posts and did not allow the Englishmen to be judged by Indian magistrates. They passed law reducing the minimum age limit for I.C.S. examination from 21 years to 19 years which went against many Indian youths.

The aforesaid acts of repression, racial discrimination and economic exploitation meted out to Indians by the British help mature the political consciousness and culminated in the founding of the Indian National Congress in 1885. Even before this, some similar organizations had been functioning in India which can be described as the trend setters of the Indian National Congress. These organizations were, the British India Association 1843 ; India

League 1875; Indian Association 1876; Bombay Association; National Conference 1883, etc. The objectives of most of these organizations were to rouse Indian awareness about the anti-India policies perpetrated by the Government of India.

Taking into account of the facts and circumstances stated above we can say that the British Rule in India not only provided political unity to the country to stand against the foreign rule but also brought to them national awakening and liberal ideas of the western world. The Indians were influenced by the democratic and efficient form of government in Great Britain and were keen to transplant the same system of administration in India. Lord Ronaldshay was correct when he said — "The young Indians drank deep the new wine of western learning and became steeped in ideas of liberty and nationalism".

Freedom Movement of India

The freedom movement of India may be said to have begun after the formation of the Indian National Congress in 1885. Throughout the past several years, India was in need of a political organization which could adequately voice against the unjust and oppressive policies adopted by the British and to safeguard the rights and interest of the Indian people. This long felt need was fulfilled by the founding of the Indian National Congress which went a long way to institutionalize the Indian nationalism. At the initial stage the Indian National Congress, though named National Congress, was mainly represented by educated middle class intelligentsia, and persons of liberal professions like lawyers, teachers, writers, etc. Most members were drawn from the cities and towns and was hardly percolated down the rural areas. They did not totally condemned the British Government but they wanted to bring reformation and remedy to certain policies of the government through negotiations. Dr. R.G. Pradhan said, "They were practical reformers imbued with the spirit, principles and methods of mid-Victorian Liberation and bent on winning freedom by gradual stages, broadening from step to step". These leaders believed that the chief obstacle in the way of India's progress was not the British rule, but the social and economic backwardness of the people. They were hopeful that if they could convince the government about their cause the British would certainly redress their grievances. The prominent leaders of this period were Dadabhai Naoroji,

Surendranath Banerjee, Phirozshah Mehta, Gopal Krishna Gokhale, M.G. Ranade, Pandit Madan Mohan Malviya, etc.

After about two decades of pursuasion policy followed by the Indian Congress having failed, the Indian leaders hardened their stance and changed the method of approach to the government. By this time the Indian nationalism had been sufficiently matured and the ideal of *Swaraj-Swabhasa-Swadharma*, propounded by Swami Dayananda Saraswati, had assumed the political colour. A crop of youths with revolutionary ideal had become restive in various parts of India under the leadership of Bal Gangadhar Tilak, Lala Lajpat Rai, B.C. Pal, etc. This younger group of politicians believed that the policy of prayer and petition would not lead them anywhere, therefore, the objective should be Swaraj (independence) and that could be achieved only through the use of arms. The extremists laid emphasis on boycott of foreign goods and promotion of Swadeshi or home made products They held a meeting at Kanpur in October 1924 and decided to set up Hindustan Socialist Republican Association (H.S.R.A.) with provincial Units in Bengal, Bihar, U.P., Delhi, Punjab and Madras. On 9th August, 1925 the U.P. revolutionists successfully carried out decoity on the Kakori bound train on the Saharanpur-Lucknow railway line. The offenders of this case, Ramprasad Bismil and Roshanlal were hanged until death. Another revolutionist Bhagat Singh shot dead Mr. Saunders, the S.P. of Lahore, on 17 December, 1928 to avenge the fatal assault on Lala Lajpat Rai during the anti-Simon Commission demonstration on 30 October, 1928. Bhagat Singh, Raj Guru and Sukhdev were arrested in another case of throwing bomb on the Central Assembly on 8 April, 1929 and later on, they were executed in Lahore jail on 23 March, 1931.

The partition of Bengal by Lord Curzon in 1905 brought about wide resentment and agitation. People launched Swadeshi movement, staged hartals and demonstration in protest against the partition. Revolutionists young men of Bengal became restive. The resentment of the revolutionists against government found outlet in the murder of Mr. B.C. Allen, the District Magistrate of Dacca in December 1907. On another occasion Khudiram Bose and Prafulla Chaki attempted on the life of Kingsford, the Judge of Muzaffarpur on April 30, 1908. Khudiram was hanged while Prafulla Chaki shot himself. The British Government dealt the revolutionists with heavy hand and put a large number of them in the prison and their movement gradually lost momentum by 1919.

It must, however, be agreed that despite the failure of the extremist movement it left a deep impact upon the ongoing nationalist movement.

Mahatma Gandhi entered Indian politics in 1917 with the *Satyagraha* movement at Champaran in Bihar. In 1918, Gandhi launched "No Tax Campaign" at Khera in Gujarat where the peasants were not able to pay the revenue because of famine condition that prevailed there. He succeeded to strike a compromise between the peasant and the government. Mahatma Gandhi called for accelerated movement for attainment of *Purna Swaraj* through truthful and non-violent methods. He appealed to the people to practice five virtues, i.e., spinning, removal of untouchability, sobriety (nonconsumption of alcohol), Hindu-Muslim unity and equality for women. The clarion call of Gandhi reached the common people living in the rural areas and the movement took the turn for mass movement. Prior to this, the Indian National Congress was limited to the middle class people of the cities and developed regions of the country. It was Gandhiji's unique role to mobilize the masses for the welfare of the country and to convert the Congress into an organization of the masses. His pursuance of truth and non-violence, simple living and eating habit, his recourse to daily prayer, love for poor and *dalits* attracted common people.

On March 30, 1919 Mahatma Gandhi started *Satyagraha* movement to protest against the Rawlatt Act 1919 which empowered the Government to put any one behind the bars, even on suspicion of disloyalty to the State without producing him before the Magistrate. There was countrywide hartals, processions and meetings purely on non-violent method. The hartals remained, by and large peaceful except in Delhi, Punjab, Gujarat and Bengal where the Government tried to suppress the movement by application of forceful means. But the people remained non-violent following the instruction of Mahatma Gandhi. Jawaharlal Nehru, dealing on the doctrine of non-violence, said, "Gandhiji had placed it before the country not only as the right method but as the most effective one for our purpose. Inspite of its negative name it was a dynamic method, the very opposite of a meek submission to tyrant will. It was not a cowardly refusal from action, but a brave man's defence of evils and national subjection". (Jawaharlal Nehru, *Autobiograpny* 1936, p.82.) The police took recourse to lathi charge, arrests and even firing in order to break the processions. The worst incident, however, took place at Jallianwala Bagh in Punjab where the army opened fire on a peaceful assembly of several thousand Indians. On April 13, 1919 at 4-30 P.M. nearly 20,000 people had gathered at a place called Jallianwala Bagh and were attending a meeting, army General O. Dyer reached there with a platoon of soldiers and in a spirit of vengeance, ordered to fire upon the innocent crowd. Hundreds of people were killed and thousands were wounded as there was no way to escape except one passage which was blocked by the army. The most inhuman act was that those dead and half dead people were left there at the place of occurrence till next morning and no one was allowed to take them as curfew was clamped around that area.

An atmosphere of panic and anguish prevailed throughout the country. The incident hardened the minds of the political leaders and became determined to make further sacrifices for the sake of the country. The annual session of the Congress held at Nagpur in December 1920 ratified the movement launched by Gandhiji. It held that "the object of the Indian National Congress is the attainment of Swaraj by the people of India by all legitimate and peaceful means". Gandhi launched non-cooperation movement in 1921 through boycott of official functions, withholding of children from schools, boycott of courts by lawyers. Ravindranath Tagore surrendered his title of 'Sir', the Indian members of the Viceroy's Council resigned from their membership. Distinguished persons like C.R. Das, Motilal Nehru, Jawaharlal Nehru, Lala Lajpat Rai and Rajendra Prasad gave up their lucrative practice at Bar and joined the non-cooperation movement. Many students gave up their studies in the Government run schools and joined Rashtriya Vidyapiths. The ongoing programme of boycotting foreign goods was intensified and taken to the villages by Congress workers. The purpose of boycotting foreign goods was to hamper Great Britain's trade of manufactured goods in India and to promote Indian industries. This was the reason why Gandhi's non-cooperation and non-violent movement easily captured the imagination of the mass people. Political leaders stopped wearing foreign clothes and used Indian handloom clothes. The use of *swadeshi* goods became popular and Khadi clothes became the symbol of patriotism.

Unfortunately for Gandhiji the incident of violence that took place at Chouri Choura brought a setback to his non-violent movement. On February 4, 1922, a group of Congress workers turn violent and set fire on the Police Station of Chauri Chaura in retaliation against the opening fire by the police on the agitating peasants. Twenty-two police men including young son of a Sub-Inspector of Police were burnt alive who were hiding inside the Police Station after their ammunitions exhausted. Gandhiji was shocked and mortally pained at this violent act committed by his own Congress workers and he suspended the non-cooperation movement forthwith. Thus, the first phase of the non-co-operation movement came to an end abruptly But though the movement failed to achieve its goal of 'Swaraj ' it succeeded in generating the support of the people at grass root level with their firm conviction that the forces of repression perpetrated by the British must end for the welfare of the country. Even a lay man from the village believed that only Swaraj could bring prosperity to India. This was not a mean achievement of Gandhiji. This fact is amply evidenced by the following comment expressed by the Intelligence Branch of the Government of India —

> "Never before has any political leader, or perhaps, even a religious leader, in his own life time stirred the masses to their very depths throughout the country and received the homage of so many people, Hindus and Muslims alike. His influence is certainly phenomenal and quite unprecedented."

In December 1929, Simon Commission was constituted by the British Parliament to probe into the functioning of the Government of India Act 1919 and to suggest to the Government its future course of action. The Commission consisted of seven members of the British Parliament, with John Simon as Chairman and not a single Indian was included as a member. This was not acceptable to India as it was a direct humiliation and underestimation of India The Indian leaders felt that the British Government had no right to decide on the matters concerning India without a single representative taken from India. Lord Irwin the Viceroy, made it clear that the British Government would permit the Indians to present their case before the British Parliament as declared by the Prime Minister. This could be done either by a Joint Committee consisting of representatives of the Central legislature and Provincial legislatures which would be permitted to put up views and proposals before the Commission, or by a delegation elected by the Indian Central Legislature could present a case after the submission of the report by the Commission. The Congress, however, preferred to stick to its previous stand. In its annual session held at Madras in December 1927, the Congress decided to boycott the 'all-white Commission'. The Hindu Mahasabha also followed the suit while the Muslim League was divided on this issue, although the majority of the members led by M.A. Jinnah was in favour of the boycott. Therefore, when, on February 7, 1928, the Commission landed in Bombay, it was greeted with a country wide hartals, demonstrations, black flags and slogans of "Simon go back". It was in one such demonstration that Lala Lajpat Rai was brutally beaten by the police due to which he died after some days. Many other Congress leaders including Jawaharlal Nehru and Ballavbhai Patel and Govind Ballav Pant were also injured.

The Lahore Annual Session of the Congress held on November 29, 1929 elected Jawaharlal Nehru as its President and at the mid-night of December 31, 1929 the Congress Committee declared *Purna Swaraj* as it goal. The Working Committee then authorized Gandhiji to launch a programme of Civil Disobedience with the ultimate aim of attaining complete independence. Accordingly on March 12, 1930 Mahatma Gandhi started Civil Disobedience movement by breaking the Salt Law and making salt at the sea beach called Dandi, a small village in Gujarat. On that day, early morning he marched from Sabarmati Ashram on foot with 78 followers and reached the sea at Dandi on April 5 where Gandhiji and his followers made salt in violation of the salt laws. The movement of Civil Disobedience spread all over the country. Salt laws were broken in many places and even women joined the movement. The Civil Disobedience movement did not confine to breaking salt law but it spread in every aspect of the government administration, laws, rules and regulations such as boycotting foreign goods, withholding payment of government taxes, land revenue, salt tax, violating restraint orders, boycotting official functions, etc. They also held meetings, took out processions against prohibitions, picketing government offices, etc. Although the Muslims largely kept themselves aloof from this movement, the *Khudai Khidmatgar* under the leadership of Khan Abdul Ghaffar Khan, dominated the movement in the N.W.F. Province. In Assam Congress leaders like Gopinath Bordoloi, Bishnuram Medhi, Omeo Kumar Das, Vijai Chanfra Bhagawati and many others led the movement from different districts. In Madras, C. Rajagopalachari led the movement and travelled on foot from Trichinapalli to Vedarayama to prepare salt on the sea coast. As the tempo of the movement grew up the Government authority rose in vengeance and dealt with merciless repression. Not less than 60,000 Congress volunteers including prominent leaders were arrested and put in prison. Among those biggest leaders were Mahatma Gandhi, Vallavbhai Patel, Jawaharlal Nehru, Rajagopalachari, Madan Mohan Malayiya, J. M. Sengupta, B. G. Kher, K. M. Munshi, etc. According to an official report 103 persons were killed, 240 injured 60,000 were imprisoned

After the Simon Commission submitted its report, the British Government called the Round Table Conference on November 12, 1930 to deliberate and discuss with the Indian leaders about the future course of action to be followed . But the Congress refused to attend the Conference, as it felt that it would be futile to discuss anything in the absence of Indian representative for the Commission in the preparation of original report of the Commission. So the first Round Table Conference was adjourned *sine die.*

The British Prime Minister, Ramsay MacDonald in an attempt to dissuade the Indian leaders from political agitation held out before them a hope of making substantial transfer of powers to India. Lord Irwin, the Viceroy of India came forward with a proposal to hold a political dialogue with Gandhiji and both of them together forged an agreement which is known as the "Gandhi-Irwin Pact". According to this Pact the Government prepared to withdraw all repressive measures and release all political prisoners except those convicted of violent crimes ; to restore the confiscated properties of the Satyagrahis ; to permit peaceful picketing and making salt free of duty to persons residing within a specific distance of the sea-shore. The Congress, on its part, agreed to suspend Civil Disobedience movement and to participate in the next Round Table Conference. Although this Pact was opposed by top Indian leaders like Jawaharlal Nehru and Subhas Chandra Bose, it was ultimately ratified by the Karachi Congress held on 30 March, 1931, which also authorized Gandhiji to represent the Congress at the forthcoming Round Table Conference.

The Second Round Table Conference met in London in September 1931 which was attended by Mahatma Gandhi. It held discussions on the recommendations of the Simon Commission and considered about new demands put up by Gandhi but failed to come to any consensus because of controversial views expressed by different members. Gandhiji became disappointed and returned empty handed. Subsequently on 1st January, 1932 the Congress met in Delhi and discussed political situation under the light of the deliberations of the last Round Table Conference and decided to resume the Civil Disobedience Movement once again. Accordingly Mahatma Gandhi announced the revival of the Civil Disobedience Movement from the same date of 1st January, 1932. The movement got under way in the right earnest, very soon the law and order broke down and tension mounted far and wide in the country. The Government stepped up its repressive measures and apprehended Gandhi and put him behind the bars. Many other provincial leaders were also taken into custody in an effort to suppress the agitation.

Mr. MacDonald, the British Prime Minister hastened to announce "MacDonald Award" on August 16, 1932 which, according to the official claim, will provide some privileges to the minority communities and *dalit* classes of people. The Award, however, proved detrimental to the national unity and integrity of India and was rejected by the people calling it as the "Communal Award". It was intended to bring about division among the Hindus, Muslims and Christians and even between the Hindu depressed and the higher caste people. The principal features of the Communal Award were as follows:

(a) Separate Electorate system would be continued.
(b) Except the North-West Frontier Province, seats would be reserved for women in every legislature.
(c) Weightage would be given to the Muslims in all provinces where they were in minority.
(d) The depressed classes were accepted as a separate minority group and were given separate representation in all legislatures.
(e) Christians and Anglo-Indians were provided separate constituencies.
(f) Labours, commercial, industrial and tea gardens' Associations were given special representations.

The Congress felt that the Award was fraught with dangers of dividing Indians into different religions, castes and classes and it was a British design to put a wedge between Indian communities and classes. Gandhiji was in Poona district jail at that time and was deeply shocked by the sinister motive of the British Prime Minister. He immediately resorted to fast from 20 September, 1932 until death or till the Award was withdrawn in 1932. The hard decision taken by Gandhiji created a great stir among the Congress leaders. They set to devise an amicable settlement to this problem and finally, at the behest of Dr. B.R. Ambedkar, the leader of the depressed classes and other Congress members of different religions succeeded to strike a solution which was known as Poona Pact. This timely solution made by Congress leaders saved the situation.

The deliberations of the third Round Table Conference finally resulted in the passing of the *Government of India Act 1935*. This Act envisaged a federation at the centre including the native States. The purpose for introduction of this Act was to provide the Provinces complete autonomy with elected legislatures of their own. Before 1935 the provinces were controlled by the centre. But under the new system each province became a responsible unit and derived its legal powers from the constitution. While it was compulsory for the provinces to join the federation, it was voluntary in the case of princely States which could join the federation by executing an instrument of accession. The Federal Executive at the centre was to be composed of the Governor-General and a Council of Ministers who were to be elected by the Governor-General and would hold office at his pleasure. The Governor-General had special responsibility in respect of certain specified subjects and in some important departments such as, Defence, Foreign Affairs, Ecclesiastical Affairs and the Administration of Tribal Areas, the Governor-General was empowered to act with the assistance of three Counsellors appointed by him.

In the provinces the Governor was the chief of executive authority and was empowered to act in his own discretion. The Act 1935 provided creation of a Council of Ministers in the province to advise the Governor who would appoint the Ministers from amongst the members of the local legislatures. In the provinces of

Assam, Bihar, Bombay, Madras and United Province, the Act provided for two legislatures each Legislative Council and Legislative Assembly. The rest of the provinces would have a single chamber named Legislative Assembly. These Assemblies were to function for a term of five years and their members were to be directly elected by people every five years.

The Second World War and Indian Politics

With the break out of the Second World War in September 1939, the freedom movement of India took a new turn. Lord Linlithgow, the Viceroy of India requested the Indian political leaders to lend their support to the Government in its war efforts. The non-Congress or the League ministers of Bengal, the Punjab and Sindh pledged support to the government. The Congress decided not to lend its support on the ground that the government did not consult with the people of India before it declared the war. The Congress severely criticized this action — Mawlana Azad commented — "The Viceroy's action proved that the British Government looked on India as a creature of its will and was not willing to recognize India's right to decide her course for itself even in a matter like war". Mahatma Gandhi expressed sympathy with the Allies who had declared that they were fighting war for safeguarding democracy, but that was his personal opinion. Subhas Chandra Bose wanted rather to take the opportunity of Britain's weakness during war and wrest freedom of India by force than to help the British. He resigned from the Congress and formed another association named Forward Block. Finally, the Congress decided to co-operate with the Government on two conditions — one, that India would be given complete independence after the war and two, that a Government consisting of all major political parties in India should be established at the centre which should be responsible to the Central legislature. The Government did not agree to this condition. The Viceroy of India, however, issued a declaration on August 8, 1940 which was known as the "August Offer". Through this declaration the Government agreed to grant Dominion Status to India after the war and also the right to frame its own constitution. As it fell short of the demand of the Congress for a Complete independent India, the Congress, after threadbare discussion, rejected the 'August Offer'. The Muslim League also rejected the 'Offer' as it did not mention giving of Pakistan.

The Satyagraha movement began once again on October 17, 1940. under the leadership of Binoba Bhave. Mahatma Gandhi observed much restraint and wanted the movement should be peaceful and should not involve mass people. In a letter to Winston Churchill, British Prime Minister, dated 1st June, 1940 Gandhiji wrote with sympathy "We do not seek our independence out of Britain's ruin". Although the individual Satyagraha did not have much impact on the Government and it continued to demonstrate the spirit of non-cooperation of the people of India with the Government.

On 11 March, 1942 Churchill announced the deputation of Sir Stafford Cripps, a member of the war Cabinet and leader of the House of Commons, on a mission to India with a generous offer Cripps arrived India at Delhi on 22 March, discussed the Draft Declaration with the leaders of all parties and published it on 29 March, 1942. The Declaration promised to give Indians the following rights and privileges:

1. India would be granted full Dominion Status and the right to secede from British Commonwealth.
2. After the war a constitution making body would be formed and elected by members of the Lower House of Provincial legislatures by proportional representation system.
3. In case of any province not agreeing to the constitution that would be accepted by the British Government giving them the same status as that of the Indian Union.
4. A treaty would be negotiated between the British Government and the constitution-making body to cover all matters arising out of the complete transfer of responsibility from British to Indian hands.
5. By the time the new constitution is framed the British government would retain the control of the defence of India through Government of India in co-operation with the people of India.

The Cripps' declaration of 'full dominion' was not acceptable for the Indian leaders on the ground that it did not bring the promise of independence which the Indian leaders wanted.

Gandhiji described it as "a Post-dated Cheque upon a crashing bank". The Congress was opposed to the novel principle of non-accession of the provinces as it struck at the very root concept of Indian unity. Cripps' proposals contained such provisions which may lead to division of India into tiny independent governments.

Quit India Movement of 1942

The failure of the Cripps' Mission on the one hand and the second World War raging on the eastern border of India, on the other, created a situation of extreme political insecurity and acute economic crisis in the country. The unwanted war was clamped upon India by the British which could have been avoided had the British left India. The rising cost of essential commodities adversely affected the life of the Indian people The war had drained off all the resources of the country. The roads, buildings, means of transport, raw materials, foodstuff, water, power and everything being requisitioned for the army, the normal life of the civilian population in the North-East became deplorable. The influx of the refugees from Burma made the situation all the more worst. The Indian political leaders believed that the sooner the British left India the better for the Indian people. Mahatma Gandhi, who was sympathetic towards the British, because of war, also disclosed his change of mind in an article in the *Harijan*. He was convinced of the necessity of starting a mass movement again. He observed, "The presence of the British in India is an invitation to Japanese to invade India. Their withdrawal removes the bait. Assume, however, it does not ; free India will be better able to cope with the invasion. Unadulterated non-cooperation will then have full sway". The Congress Working Committee met at Wardha in July and demanded immediate withdrawal of the British from India. Finally, on August 18, 1942, the All India Congress Committee in its meeting held at Bombay ratified the *Quit India* resolution. The resolution read — "The immediate ending of the British Rule in India is an urgent necessity for India. That a provisional government will be formed .... Its primary function must be to defend India .... The Provisional government will evolve a scheme for a Constituent Assembly". (L.P. Sarma, *Indian National Movement*, 1996-97, p. 164) The Congress working Committee endorsed the starting of a mass struggle on non-violent lines, on the widest possible scale, to convince the British that they should quit India immediately. Mahatma Gandhi was entrusted with the sole authority and leadership of the movement. The Government was fully aware of the political development that was taking place in the Congress camps and was accordingly prepared to contain the emerging situation. On August 9, 1942, all the members of the Congress Working Committee including Gandhiji were arrested early in the morning before they woke up and were put behind the bars. The Congress party was also declared illegal organization. Subsequently after the Quit India movement got under way other Congress members were also arrested and put in prison. But the people took up the challenge and came out into the street and joined in hartal, processions and demonstrations. The British presumption that in the absence of leaders the movement would automatically die down, proved wrong. Under the leadership of the district and local Congress the schools and colleges were closed down and the teachers and the students took part in the movement. Although the Congress leaders tried to adopt non-violent method the movement could not remain so. On many occasions the demonstrators and Congress volunteers disrupted transport services, broke down communication systems, took possession of Railway stations and even tried to trespass into police stations. The police, on their part, lathi charged on the volunteers, burst tear gas shells, snatched away Congress flags and banners, and at times opened fires on the crowd killing many people.

In Assam the Quit India movement was launched vigorously. A fifteen years old school girl named Kanaklata Baruah was killed on police firing and another Kushal Konwar was hanged to death during the movement. Holding of meetings, taking out processions, shouting slogans *"Vandemataram"*, *Inqilab Jindabad"*, *"Karenge yaa Marenge"*, etc., and trying to hoist Congress flags at police stations were everyday features. Many students joined *Mukti Bahini* and *Mrityu Bahini* and took active part in various types of subversive acts. I was a student of class seven at that time and I was given the role of carrying secret letters and communication to and from the Congress leaders who were in the hiding to evade arrest. These leaders were mainly responsible in conducting the movement by issuing instructions and guidance from their hideouts, while the movement was spearheaded mostly by the students, peasants and people of middle class. Although the Government brought down the agitation with heavy hand and the non-violent and subversive activities came to grinding halt within two months, the underground movement continued till the beginning of 1943. According to an estimate nearly 26,000 persons were arrested and the police fired 530 rounds resulting in the death of nearly 940 people and injuring about 1630. (L.P.Sarma, *Indian National Movement*, p. 165)

The Quit India movement failed because it lacked organisation and leadership. The movement also did not receive support from many sections of the society and political parties. The Communist Party of India advocated withdrawal of the movement because it supported Russia which was an allied power with Great Britain. The Muslim League also opposed the Quit India Movement. Dr. B.R. Ambedkar, the veteran leader of the *dalits*, described the movements "Irresponsible and an act of madness". Many business houses, the army, the bureaucrats, and the police actively helped the government in suppressing the agitation.

However, the massive Quit India movement of 1942 made it clear to the British that the Indians were by now fully conscious of their political rights and the they were determined to be free from any foreign rule. Apart from this, the war of independence fought in Burma by the Indian National Army (Azad Hind Fauz) under the political leader, Netaji Subhas Chandra Bose sent a positive message to the British Government that the Indian soldiers on whose strength the colonial government stood, were no longer with them. Therefore, eventually Lord Attlee, the British Prime Minister made an announcement in the floor of the House of Commons that Britain would leave India by June, 1948. Accordingly, on the midnight of August, 1947, India became independent.

4

Gorkhas in Freedom Movement of India

In the wake of India's struggle for freedom during 1920s when the people of India, irrespective of caste, creed and religion, joined hands together under the leadership of Mahatma Gandhi, the Gorkhas living in different parts of India could not remain aloof. No doubt, they were educationally backward, socially and economically weak but these factors did not deter them from joining the bandwagon of national main stream. Initially the elite section of the Gorkhas from Darjeeling, Calcutta, Banaras and Dehradun spearheaded the cause of nationalist movement through separate organizations. The pioneering among them were — the Hillmen Association of Darjeeling formed in 1921, the Gorkha Association of Calcutta formed in 1926, and the All India Gorkha League established in 1921 at Dehradun. Through the platforms of these organizations the leaders of Indian Gorkhas took the cudgels of arousing national awareness among the Indian Nepalis. Side by side with the activities of these socio-political organizations the press also took its own role to educate people by publication of various news magazines and periodicals in Nepali language. The pioneers among them were the *Gorkha Sathi* from Calcutta (1911), the *Gorkhali* and *Janma-bhumi* from Banaras (1914 and 1921 respectively), the *Tarun Gorkha* from Dehradun (1927). The Nepali periodicals, besides writing on social and cultural aspects, published articles on Mahatma Gandhi's doctrine of non-violence and non-co-operation and *Swadeshi* movement and instilled feeling of nationalism among the Gorkhas. The British Government was, however, extremely careful to see that the seed of nationalism did not grow among the Indian Gorkhas, who produced the Gorkha recruits for Indian army. British wanted that the Gorkha young boys should not be adulterated by political ideologies which might erode their loyalty to the Crown and, therefore, they kept strict vigilance on them. One Nepali periodical named *Gorkhali* was proscribed by Government of India in 1922 under Indian Vernacular Press Act 1910 on the suspicion that it disseminated nationalist ideas among the Gorkhas. Another Nepali news-magazine was ordered to deposit security for maintenance of good behaviour under the same Press Act, as a result of which it ceased to publish at all. Strict confidential instructions were issued by the Government of India, from time to time, to all Deputy Commissioners and Superintendents of Police to keep close watch on the political activities of Indian Gorkhas and to prevent them from indulging in politics

Despite these strict precautionary measures taken by the Government, clandestine political activities continued to be carried out by elite Gorkha young men infiltrating political ideas into the areas of Nepalis concentration. The echoes of Mahatma Gandhi's clarion call for non-co-operation movement, found their ways into the hills and plains of India. In Darjeeling, a good number of Gorkhas joined the Indian National Congress and took active part in *Satyagraha* movement under the guidance of Nepali leaders like Dal Bahadur Giri, Jonbir Sapkota and Prithiman Lama. Mahatma Gandhi's visit to Darjeeling in 1921 brought about a new enthusiasm among the Gorkhas who met him personally and became influenced by him.[1] (S.K. Singh, *Tribal Movement in India*, p. 342) A political leader Bhagat Bir Tamang was arrested and severely beaten by police for his active participation in the non-co-operation movement and put in prison where he died in 1923. He was the first political martyr among the Nepalis in India.

In Calcutta, the hub of the Revolutionary group of national activists, Gorkha youths coming from various parts of India and Nepal for study were inspired by the firebrand leaders like Aurobindo Ghose, Bhupendranath Dutta, Rash Behari Bose, Prafulla Chaki, etc., who wanted to wrest freedom from the hands of the British by violent means. They believed in armed conflict against the British Government with the help of Indian soldiers working in the Indian army. For this purpose a group of Gorkhas under the leadership of Khadak Bahadur Bist, a law student of Calcutta University and General Secretary of Calcutta Gorkha League, had established secret nexus with army cantonment to enlist support of Gorkha soldiers. In June 1930, while engaged in this clandestine work Khadak Bahadur and Dhanapati Singh a

Gorkha soldier were arrested and jailed. Later, Dhanapati Singh was dismissed from his military service as an exemplary punishment. Another Gorkha soldier Prithiman Thapa deserted his service and joined the revolutionary group of Bengal and continued to carry on secret political activities. Khadak Bahadur Bist was arrested in May 1930 for attempting to loot the Government salt depot at Dharsana together with 13 others, 150 miles from Bombay and was imprisoned at Sabarmati jail with his thirteen Gorkha associates. After his release from Sabarmati jail he continued his political activities of secretly enticing Gorkha soldiers for revolutionary works. Khadak Bahadur Bist was a close associate of Sachindra Sanyal, revolutionary leader of Bengal who mentioned in his autobiography that contacts were established with the Indian soldiers of the Army Cantonments of North India from where many Gorkha soldiers agreed to join the revolutionary party. Later on, Khadak Bahadur was once again arrested and the police recovered from his possession many incriminating documents including a list of Gorkha soldiers willing to join freedom movement. Since 1943 Khadak Bahadur Bist was found missing from his home and since that time he has never been seen nor his whereabouts is known. His missing from this country is still a mystery.

The Indian Gorkhas were also inspired by the political leaders of Nepal who crossed over to India for political asylum during their anti-Rana activities of 1920s. One Krishna Prasad Koirala came to settle in Benaras after he was exiled by the Rana Government. Together with him came his two sons, Matrika Prasad Koirala and Biseswar Prasad Koirala, who were to become the two leading protagonists in Nepalese politics in course of time. In 1950s after the autocratic Rana Government was overthrown both the brothers were elected as the Prime Ministers of Nepal one after another. In 1920-21 Krishna Prasad Koirala together with Ramkrishnalal Shrestha, Ram Chandra Adhikari and many other Gorkhas of Benaras actively participated in *Swadeshi* movement and burnt foreign clothes. It was said that the heap of the imported garments burnt by the Gorkhas at Maidagil ground of Benaras was the biggest of all the heaps of clothes burnt by other communities.[2] (B.L. Upadhyaya, *Khanmihali*, 2004, p.126). At that time Matrika Prasad and Biseswar Prasad were students of High English School and they were shifted to Rashtriya Vidyalaya so as to comply with the call of the Swadeshi movement which decided to boycott English language, foreign goods, honorary offices under the Government and membership of Legislative Council.[3] (L. P. Sarma, *Indian National Movement*, p. 98). Ramkrishnalal Shrestha was the President of the Benaras City Congress and Krishna Prasad Koirala and other Gorkhas of Benaras were members.

Later on Krishna Prasad Koirala and his family moved to Pratapgarh in the district of Bhagalpur in Bihar and settled down there. There he continued his political career and became the member of the Bhagalpur district Congress Committee and the President of the Pratapgarh Thana Congress Committee. As the time passed, his son Matrika Prasad Koirala became an active member of the Indian National Congress. In 1926, he came to Assam to attend the All India Congress Conference held at Pandu as a delegate. He became the General Secretary of Patna District Congress Committee and also held the office of the Joint Secretary of Bihar Provincial Committee for launching movement against the Simon Commission. The Congress had decided to boycott the Simon Commission in 1927 which was constituted by the British Government with seven members of the British Parliament with Sir John Simon as its Chairman, all white members, without a single member from India. It was for this reason that the Congress leaders decided to boycott the Simon Commission.

His brother, Biseswar Prasad Koirala also took active part in Indian politics and suffered imprisonment for four years at different jails in India. He met Dr. Rajendra Prasad (Later the President of India) as a co-prisoner at Bankipur jail in 1930 and later on he was shifted to Hazaribagh jail where he met Jagjivan Ram, who became the Defence Minister and Deputy Prime Minister of India after India became independent. During these days of political turmoil he established very intimate relations with the top socialist leaders of India like Jaiprakash Narayan, Dr. Ram Manohar Lohia, Acharya Kripalani, etc. His father, Ram Krishna Koirala at his old age returned back to Nepal only to be arrested on the charge of harbouring Indian political leaders who fled to Nepal during Quit India Movement in 1942. He was put behind the bars where he breathed his last. At this time Biseswar Prasad Koirala was in Hazaribagh jail in India and was not allowed to visit his bereaved mother and family in Nepal.

The freedom movement of India proved as a training ground for the Nepalese leaders to learn politics against the autocratic Rana rulers in Nepal. They not only learnt the techniques of political movement from the veteran leaders of India like Mahatma Gandhi, Jaiprakash Narayan, Dr. Ram Manohar Lohia, etc., but also continued to receive constant guidance and inspirations from them during the civil movement in Nepal. To cite an instance, in 1935 a group of elite Nepalese young men, under the leadership of Pandit Shukra Raj Shastri formed an association named Nepali Praja Parishad. A delegation of this organisation consisting of Shukra Raj Shastri, Gangalal and Dharma Bhakta met Mahatma Gandhi and Dr. Ram Manohar Lohia in India and after receiving necessary guidance and blessings from Mahatma Gandhi they returned back to Nepal. But no sooner than they had set their feet on the soil of Nepal they were arrested and put in jail by the Nepalese Government. The intelligence network of the Nepalese Government was in close liaison with its counterpart in the Government of British India which passed quick information about the whereabouts of these Nepalese leaders. By the first October 1940, Narashamsher Rana, the Director General of Police arrested nearly 500 Nepalese insurgents under the charges of conspiracy for waging war against the Rana Government and put them into the prison cell. After a brief trial Yudh Shamsher Rana, the Prime Minister of Nepal pronounced the final judgement of the case in the Singha Darbar before a jampacked audience which included top civil and military officials. According to the judgement order: Shukra Raj Shastri, Dasarath Chand, Dharma Bhakta, Gangalal and Subba Puran Chandra were found guilty of treason and conspiracy against the Government and awarded death sentences with appropriation of their properties; Tek Prasad Upadhyaya, Ram Hari and Sankar Prasad Sarma were awarded life imprisonment, appropriation of properties and excommunication. The other twenty-six accused persons were awarded imprisonment of various lengths and severities while the rest of the arrested persons were acquitted. This historic event sent the message of shock and terror down the hills and valleys of Nepal. After a period of two months, on the fateful day came of 30th January, 1941, — early morning, the above named five gallant patriots of Nepal were executed in open public view. With this ended the anti-Rana movement of Nepal never to resurrect again in the soil of the Himalayan kingdom for a considerable time. This historic day of 30th January, 1941 will be remembered forever by the people of Nepal as a *Black Day* in the annals of democratic movement in Nepal.

The exemplary role played by the Nepalese political leaders in the freedom movement of India had a direct impact on the Indian Gorkhas. The clarion call of *Swadashi* movement given by Swami Dayananda Saraswati and the *Satyagraha* movement of Mahatma Gandhi reached the nooks and corners of the country. The Gorkhas who had been living for generations in the hills and plains of the North-East responded magnificently to the call and joined hands together with other local Indians. Their real political movement was, however, triggered by an incident that took place in 1920 when, on one fateful day a battery of Forest officials, accompanied by armed police arrived at the scene, and set fire the cattlesheds and dwelling houses of Nepali graziers of Kajiranga numbering hundred and one families. Within minutes, their dwelling houses and cattlesheds, including their household goods and wearing apparels turned into heaps of ashes. No prior notice was served nor a reasonable time was allowed to them to salvage their household goods. These Nepali graziers had been living there peacefully for more than fifty years paying grazing fees to the government at stipulated rates per head of cattle. Such an unjust and inhuman act of the British Government mortally hurt the sentiment of the loyal and peaceful Gorkhas. They became disillusioned and rebellious and looked for a course of action that would provide them with collective security. Finally they decided to come under the banner of the political organization under the leadership of Babu Chabilal Upadhyaya, Chandranath Sarma, Ramlal Upadhyaya, Bogiram Saikia, Hari Prasad Upadhyaya, etc.

A historic meeting of the 'Assam Association' held at Jorhat on 17th April, 1921 marked the turning point of the political history of Assam. The meeting was presided over by Babu Chhabilal Upadhyaya which adopted historic decision to merge the 'Assam Association' with All India Congress Committee and to launch the non-cooperation movement of Mahatma Gandhi in a stronger and wider parameter. The meeting also decided to bring the Gorkhas of Assam under the fold of the Congress and to take up the issue of Kajiranga eviction of graziers with the Government of

Assam. The Gorkhas joined the National Congress under the leadership of Babu Chhabilal Upadhyaya, and Assamese leaders like Tarunram Phukan, Nabin Chandra Bardoloi, Dr. Hem Chandra Baruah, Amiya Kumar Das, Kuladhar Chaliha, Gopinath Bordoloi, etc. The Gorkhas actively took part in the non-cooperation movement of 1921 protesting against the repressive measures taken by government and the heinous killing of innocent people at Jalianwalla Bag on 13 April, 1919. They boycotted foreign clothes, used home woven clothes, helped collection of Tilak Swaraj Fund, boycott of offices, schools and colleges. Babu Chhabilal Upadhyaya was a real Gandhian leader with Khadi kurta and knee-length dhoti. He took the leadership of the Nepali community of Assam during non-co-operation movement of Mahatma Gandhi in 1921. He was arrested and imprisoned in Tezpur jail for six months for taking part in non-co-operation movement. His younger brother, Hari Prasad Upadhyaya was also imprisoned for the same offence for three months.

Dalbir Singh Lohar was another Gorkha leader from Dibrugarh, Assam who started his political career as Congress volunteer as early as he was a school student. In 1930 he suffered imprisonment for three months for joining the agitation against the Cunninghum Circular, a political issue raised by the National Congress. During the period of Civil Disobedience movement in 1930 he was arrested for the second time and was detained in Dibrugarh jail for two months. Dalbir Singh Lohar was known for his close association with Labour Union as its leader. He was the President of the Dibrugarh Circle Tea Workers' Union and also the Vice President of the Assam Branch of the Indian National Trade Union Congress (INTUC). He also held the responsible office of the All Assam State Transport Workers' Association. He was elected as member of the Assam Legislative Assembly from Soikhowa constituency of Dibrugarh district during the first general election held in 1952.

Bhakta Bahadur Pradhan of Dibrugarh joined Congress in 1934. He was an active leader of the Assam Oil Company Labour Union. He met Jawaharlal Nehru for the first time when he visited Dibrugarh and was greatly influenced by his speech, delivered at the Jubilee Field, Dibrugarh. He lost his service as Motor Mechanic and Fitter in the Assam Oil Company for his involvement in the Labour Union strike. In December 1940 Bhakta Bahadur Pradhan was expelled from Assam by an order of the Governor of Assam. He was ordered to leave Assam within 72 hours and was prohibited from entering the districts of Lakhimpur, Sibsagar, Darrang and Kamrup under sub-rule (1) Clause (C) of Rule 26 of the Defence of India Rules. This was done "with a view to preventing him from acting in a manner prejudicial to the defence of British India and maintenance of public order". In 1942 he was imprisoned at Dibrugarh jail for one year for taking part in the freedom movement. After India became independent he was awarded *"Tamrapatra"* by the Chief Minister of Assam as a token of gratitude for the sacrifice made by him in bringing freedom to India.

During Quit India movement of 1942 all the top leaders of India were arrested including Mahatma Gandhi and members of the Congress Working Committee. The Indian National Congress was declared an illegal organization. But the people took up the challenge. Throughout the length and breadth of the country a mass movement was organized boycotting government offices, closing schools and colleges and taking out demonstrations demanding the British to quit India. The Gorkhas of Assam participated in the movement in large number. They resorted to hartals, processions and mass meetings. The Government banned them all and imposed restriction of assembly of more than five persons under Section of 144 Civil Procedure Code. The public meetings, and processions were forcibly dispersed, and lathi charged. The Gorkhas held meetings defying the restriction as a result of which they suffered imprisonment in different jails of Assam. Among those who were imprisoned were, Babu Chhabilal Upadhyaya, Dalbir Singh Lohar, Bhakta Bahadur Pradhan, Ramlal Upadhyaya, Bishnulal Upadhyaya, Jainarayan Upadhyaya, Kashinath Luitel, Homnath Guragain, etc. More than three hundred young Gorkha volunteers were recruited in 'Santisena' and 'Mrityu Bahini'who joined processions leading to police stations shouting slogans like, *'Bonde Mataram'*, *'Inqilab Jindabad'*, *'Karenge yaa Marenge'* etc. On many occasions the police prevented the processionists from entering into police station compound, snatched National Congress flags and lathicharged on the crowd and sometimes opened fires.

In the hole of Assam, the district of Darrang had the largest concentration of Nepalis who actively participated in the 'Quit

India' movement at various places in collaboration with the local Assamese people. They had well organized 'Mrityu-Bahinis' and 'Shati-Bahinis' raised from young boys and girls (mostly students of class IX and X) who were imparted training of drill, self defence and discipline by the Commanders. Advocate, Mohikanta Das of Tezpur was the Commander-in-Chief of the Mrityu Bahini for the whole district of Darrang and Tarun Chandra Sarma was the Organizer of it. The cadets wore Gandhi caps and badges written 'Do or Die' while their Commanders wore light grey coloured uniforms, badges and Gandhi caps. At Behali Mauja (Tehsil), the 'Mrityu-Bahini and Shanti-Bahini were trained and commanded by Padma Kanta Mahanta, Rabiram Saikia, Baneswar Dutta. On 20th September, 1942 a huge crowd consisting of more than two thousand people from surrounding villages like Majgoan, Bahbari, Hatibandha, Nakania, etc., collected at the playground of Behali High School from where a procession was taken out under the leadership of Chhabilal Upadhyaya, Bogiram Saikia, Bishnulal Upadhyaya, Kumud Chandra Sarma, Srimati Bhogmaya Devi, Annapurna Devi, Tileswari Devi and many other men, women and children. I was a twelve years boy; though not admitted in the Shanti-Bahini, I joined the crowd. The procession moved towards the Behali Police Station situated at a distance of three Km. shouting slogans and singing marching songs — "*Viswa vijayee navajawaan* — "The one and only goal of the processionists was to unfurl the Indian National Congress flag on the top of the Police Station. The procession was headed by the girls cadets closely followed by boys' catets and one cadet of each group held the Congress flags up in the air. As the crowd reached the Thana and poured into its sprawling compound they were joined by another procession which came fr5om Rangsali, Bedeti and Botiamari villages and joined sea of humanity. In the mean time, the officer-in-charge of the Police Station who was ready to meet the situation with this men in arms and lathis, warned the crowd in stern voice not to proceed further towards the Thana. The corwd, not caring the warning, pushed forward rending the sky with slogan — "*bende mataram*", "*karenge yaa marenge*", and there was a tussle between the two sides. The police lathi charged on the corwd, many volunteers were injured, some of them severely. Some of the police also suffered injuries and yet the Daroga controlled himself and refrained from resorting to firing. After abou half an hour of brawl the crowd gave up, having been called back by their leaders. The injured were carried to hospital for treatment.

From the next day the police started the campaign of arresting the leaders who participated in the procession. They arrested Chhabilal Upadhyaya, Bagiram Saikia, Bishnulal Upadhyaya, Molan Chandra Sarma, Keshav Chandra Sarma, Rabiram Saikia, Padma Kanta Mahanta, Beneswar Saikia, Dr. Annada Prasanna Datta, etc. After a few days some of them were released against whom evidences were not found, but the main leaders wee setenced to imprisonment for different lengths of time.

On the same day of 20th September the Nepalis of Helem, Gamiri, Dipura, Teleni, etc. in collaboration with local Assamese people marched to Gahapur and tried to plant Indian National congress flag at the Police Satation. Among the Nepali valunteers there were Pravakar Adhikari, Kashinath Dahal, Tikaram Bhatarai, Gobinda Pokhrel, Narapati Upadhyaya, etc. During the process of entering the Thana there was a clash between the police and the crowd leading to great turmoil in whic the police opened fire killing instantly a young girl named Kanak Lata and injuring two Nepali youths named Dambar Bhandari and Prabhakar Adhikari.

In the same way, at other places like Biswanath Chariali, Sotea and Jamuguri also the Nepalis participated in the 'Quit India' movement in large numbers and joined hands with the local Assamese people in the processions on 20 September, 1942. Some of the Nepalis who joined the Mrityu Bahini were — Khadananda Parajuli, Dilliram Sapkota, Chhabilal Gajurel, Mahindra Kafla, Tikaram Upadhyaya and Ramji Genewali.

At Tezpur, the District Headquaters of Darrang district, the resident Nepalis of the town and the graziers of Budachhapari came undr the banner of the Congress Party through their leader Prasad Singh Subba who wa sthe President of the Tezpur Graziers Association and Congress leader. The Nepali graziers used to supply milk to the whole town of Tezpur. They were directly influenced by State level Congress leades like Madhav Sarma, Kamala Prasad Agarwalla, Mohi Kanta Das, Sarma, Kamala Prasad Agarwalla, Mohi Kanta Das, Omeo Kumar Das Vijay Chandra Bhagavati, etc. On 20th September, 1942 a great number of Nepali volunteers joined the procession which was led by Tarun Chandra Sarma, the District Organizer of the Mrityu Bahini.

Under Dhekiajuli Police Station there was a large concentration of Nepalis in surrounding villages who were well organized under the leadership of Prajapati Rijal and Khemraj Rijal, the President and the Secretary of the Congress Unit of Teligoan. There was also a strong Santisena Bahini at Teligoan with many members under the command of Shri Amen Basnet. On 20th September, 1942 a huge procession consisting of all communities of the locality reached the Police Station. While trying to unfurl the National Congress flag there was a clash with the police who not onbly lathi charged on the crowd but also opened fire which killed as many as thirteen Congress volunteers and inuured many people. Among the dead were — Tileswari Baruah, Kumali Devi, Khanuli Nath, Manbar Nath, Maniram Kachari, Ratan Kachari, Mahiram Koch, Saruram Sutia, Dayal Das, Mangal Kukulur and three others. Two Nepali leaders — Hom Nath Guragai and Kashinath Luitel were arrested and put in prison for three months.

Dehradun, the hive of enlightened Gorkha ex-servicemen, was quick to be involved into the freedom movement of India from its very early stage . Being the part of erstwhile Nepalese territory till the Treaty of Sigoul: (!816), Dehradun contained a good number of original Nepalese from Terai besides the ex-servicemen of British creation. At a later stage, some non-privileged Rana families migrated to Dehradun and around the neighbouring districts in order to settle down in business. From the early beginning of the twentieth century the Gorkhas of Dehradun evinced keen interest in the Arya Samaj movement led by Swami Dayananda Saraswati whose doctrine of *Swaraja, Swabhasa and Swadharma* attracted the Gorkhas. This concept of *Swaraja* which means 'Self Rule' was converted into the political theme later on by C.R.Das and Pt. Motilal Nehru who formed another political party called Congress-Khilafat Swaraj Party. In 1924, when Gandhiji was released from imprisonment he gave his silent consent to the working of the Swarajists and both parties worked together side by side with the common goal of India's freedom.

Madan Singh Gorkha was the first person to spearhead the cause of Arya Samaj movement who played a leading role as the Secretary and later as President of Dehradun Arya Samaj from 1902 to 1907. Through this organization they came under the influence of great national leader like Lala Lajpat Rai who sowed the seed of socio-religious and political awareness among the Gorkhas of Dehradun. In 1921 they formed All India Gorkha League which was initially led and dominated by Gorkha ex-servicemen and in course of time the organization covered the whole of India. Thakur Chandan Singh, the firebrand President of the Gorkha League was an ex-serviceman who took part in the World War I and earned laurels for bravery. He belonged to Class 'C' of non-privileged Rana family and was the son-in-law of Khadak Shamsher, the brother of Chandra Shamsher, the Prime Minister of Nepal. More specifically, Gorkha League had majority of its members from among the 11,000 and odd disgruntled ex-army personnel whose names were struck off from the army roll as a measure of peace time retrenchment after the end of the World War I and who bore deep grudge against the British Government. They voiced their demands, among others, were to refrain from using the Gorkha soldiers in suppressing the Indian freedom movement and to stop classifying Gorkha soldiers into separate Gorkha Battalions on the basis of caste. It may be noted that the British Government followed the policy of classifying Gorkha soldiers into mertial and non-martial groups and organizing separate Gorkha battalions based on castes with a view to breed disunity and ill-feeling among them. This act of the British Government was not acceptable to the Gorkha soldiers at large.

Gopal Singh Thapa a retired personnel of the Survey of India and a dedicated social worker of Dehradun, sacrificed everything of his life in the freedom movement. He was imprisoned several times and his pension on which his family depended was confiscated by the British Government. He established "Tapovan" at Nalapani with all his heart and soul which is presently under the charge of the Arya Samaj. Another staunch Congress worker Dhruba Singn Thapa suffered severe police atrocities, got his house and property confiscated, lost his wife while in prison and after his release from jail, he spent the rest of his life in abject poverty sharing a room in the Congress office.

In 1930s when the Civil Disobedience Movement launched by Mahatma Gandhi swept the country the Gorkhas of Dehradun, Nalapani and Delhi rose to the occasion and rallied under the banner of the Indian National Congress. Gorkha leaders like Dhruba Singh Thapa, Riths Singh, Hukum Singh, Dal Bahadur

Thapa Lalbir Newar, etc. together with other Gorkha men, women and children held picketings and demonstrations and courted arrest. While in prison, living together with Pandit Nehru they were so much influenced that after their release from jail they changed the name of their village from Grant No.8 to Nehrugram as a mark of their love and esteem to their great leader. During mass picketing of government offices and government institutions in Delhi by Mahatma Gandhi in 1930 Khadga Bahadur Bist and Dhruba Singh Thapa together with thirty other Gorkha associates suffered imprisonment. Again in the historic Dharapani movement fifty numbers of Gorkhas were arrested and lodged in jail.

References

1. Singh, S.K. *Tribal Movement in India*, p. 342.
2. Upadhyaya B.L. *Khanmihali*, 2004, p. 126.
3. Sarma L.P. *Indian National Movement* p. 98.

5

The Gorkhas' Role in the Indian National Army

The Gorkhas' participation in the Indian National Army (INA) is one of the significant annals in the history of India's freedom movement which, unfortunately, has not received due and adequate attention of Indian historians. Many books and articles about the INA (Azad Hind Fauz) have been written by Indian and English writers, but very few have focused on the sterling role played by the Gorkha soldiers. Many movies as well as visual and electronic medias have also projected on the legendary role played by the Indian soldiers in the Azad Hind Fauz, but very little or nothing at all, has ever been highlighted about the Gorkhas who made supreme sacrifice by their lives for the liberation of India from British yoke. European and American writers like Geoffrey Tyson (*Forgotten Frontiers*, 1945), Field Marshal Willian Slim (*Defeat into Victory*, 1956), Arthur Campbell (*The Sieze : A Story from Kohima*, 1956), etc., have given a volume of information on INA but none of them have spoken about the role played by Gorkhas in the INA. Stephen P. Cohen (*The Indian Army*, 1971) has drawn but a sketchy picture of the INA. Peter Harclerode and David Reynolds (Gurkha, 2003, Gloucestershire, p.44) has referred to INA and said, "Only 26 members of the 2/2 Grorkha Rifles, led by Dhan Bahadur Rana joined the INA, when later posted to Burma, they promptly deserted". Byron Farwell (*The Gurkhas*, 1984) has flatly denied Gorkhas having participated in the INA except by one Durga Singh Lama who is said to have been hanged to death by the British. He writes :

> "Many Indians did succumb and joined the INA but no Gurkha joined. In fact, in the entire course of war

> although some 20,000 Indian changed sides, only one Gurkha, Durga Singh Lama, a former line boy, born in India, did so. Later he was captured by the British and was brought to Delhi and hanged to death after a short trial. The Gurkha prisoners were treated brutally, put in solitary confinement without food and badly beaten, still no one joined the INA". (Byron Farwell, *The Gurkhas*, 1984, p.192)

This is an outright travesty of truth as it will appear from the facts and evidences that are discussed in the paragraphs below. It was Durga Malla, and not Durga Singh Lama, as stated by Farewell, who was captured by the British army and later hanged to death in Delhi and it was also not a fact that he was the only Gorkha who joined the INA but they were there by the thousands. Historicity demands that any event of history should be treated fully and entirely and should not be left incomplete, therefore, this important aspect of the Indian history which has so far been left unwritten and unspoken and almost unknown to many people needs to be researched and brought to light. In the next paragraphs an attempt has been made to deal, at some length, on the involvement of the Gorkha soldiers in the INA under Subhas Chandra Bose and their supreme sacrifices for the noble cause of liberating their motherland from the foreign control.

The ideological conflict

India's struggle for freedom was a unique event in the history of India in the sense that towards the close of the movement there was a vertical split in its ideology into two, i.e., one was based on the principle of non-violence or *'Satyagraha'* advocated by Mahatma Gandhi and the other was founded on the bed-rock of violence under the leadership of Netaji Subhas Chandra Bose. The former believed in achieving freedom by means of nationalist movement of the mass people of India from within the country while the latter aimed at bringing a violent and abrupt end to the colonial rule through use of arms from outside with the help of foreign country. This Gandhi-Bose ideological conflict had had an enormous impact on the unity and strength of the Indian National

Congress at the important juncture of the threat of Second World War. The political situation of Indian National Congress had already been mired by the Congress-Muslim League controversy. As the cloud of the World War II grew thicker on the western horizon Subhas Chandra Bose found it as an opportunity to take advantage of the British weakness. He pleaded before the Congress leaders that India should take full advantage of the impending war to force the British out of India. Mahatma Gandhi was not in favour of this proposal. On the contrary, Gandhi supported the war efforts of the Britain and France, while the Congress as an organization stood behind Mahatma Gandhi, the undisputed leader at that time. Nehru followed the ideology of Gandhi. The advent of the Second World War and the incursion of the Japanese army on the frontiers of Burma brought the Gandhi-Bose controversy to its breaking point. Subhas Bose resigned from the office of the President of Indian National Congress and announced the formation of Forward Block a revolutionary political party within the Congress in 1939.

On January 19, 1941 Subhas Chandra Bose gave a slip to the police on guard of his house and journeyed to Peshawar with the assistance of his nephew Sisir Kumar Bose. He crossed over India's North-East Frontier and travelled through Afghanistan in disguise of a Pathan with his beards grown and pretending to be a deaf and dumb as he could not speak Pashto. He reached Moscow and had parleys for military alliance against British for India's independence, thinking that Soviet Russia, the eternal enemy of Great Britain, would hopefully agree to his proposal. But not finding encouraging response from Russian government he approached the German Ambassador in Moscow who had Bose flown to Berlin in a special courier aircraft on April 12, 1941. In Germany he had a series of secret talks with Adolf Hitler and having obtained a favourable response from him Subhas Bose founded a Free India Center in Berlin and raised a small force known as Indian Legion out of the 4,500 Indian prisoners of war who had been previously captured by the Axis forces. But the things did not move there as speedily as Subhas Bose would have wanted and the lackadaisical attitude shown by Hitler raised palpable doubts in the heart of Bose about Hitler's sincerity of the agreement. Bose left Berlin by a German sub-marine U180 *via* Cape of Good Hope and reached Tokyo on 11 May, 1943. He met the

Japanese Prime Minister Tojo who was very impressed by the proposal made by Subhas Bose. He immediately held the Japanese Parliament where he declared — "We are determined to extend every possible assistance to the cause of India's independence. It is our belief that the day is not far off when India will enjoy freedom and prosperity after attaining independence". By that time the Japanese army had already launched an offensive in the hills of Burma and Rangoon and captured a huge number of Indian soldiers in a series of wars in the Burma-Siam region. The Japanese had a plan to attack British India from the eastern frontier, and for the success of this mission the proposal of Subhas Bose for military alliance looked very meaningful for Japan. Subhas Bose, therefore, had no difficulty in convincing Emperor Hirohito and the Japanese army chief about the sincerity of his approach and to obtain Japanese consent to his proposal. Japan readily agreed to help Bose with the Indian prisoners of war, captured in Burma and necessary arms and ammunition to fight jointly against the British for the liberation of India from the colonial rule.

The Japanese army together with Subhas Bose prepared detailed plan and strategies to attack Burma and then to enter India *via* Kohima and Imphal in order to seize Brahmaputra valley. The Burma Eastern Zone was given under the command of Lieutenant General Masakazu Kawabe. The central part of Burma stretching up to Imphal Zone was placed under Lieutenant General Renya Mutaguchi who was assigned the responsibility to cross over to Assam and attack Imphal. The capture of Imphal and Kohima was a very significant strategy that was designed to stop further construction of Ledo road to link India with China which was undertaken by the American led Northern Combat Area Command. It was also agreed upon with Subhas Bose that the INA will fight jointly with the Japanese army under the command of their own officers in all these fronts and that it will take the lead in the attack of Imphal and Kohima. Subhas Bose had made the point clear that the first drop of blood that will fall on the soil of India should be that of an Indian soldier. This was the main plan of the Japanese which they named, 'U-Go Plan' or 'Operation-C' . In order to achieve this objective the following army detailment plan was prepared by the Japanese army.

1. The Japanese 33 Infantry Division under Lieutenant

General Genzo Yanagita would surround and destroy the 17th Indian Division of Tiddim and proceed to capture Imphal from the south.

2. The Japanese 33 Division Infantry under Major General Tsunonu Yamamoto would take on the 20th Division at Tamu then attack Imphal from the east. This was a heavy Infantry Division supported by 14th Tank regiment equipped with 66 assorted Tanks under Lieutenant Colonel Nobuo Ueda.
3. Another column of 15th Infantry under Lieutenant General Masafumi Yamouchi would proceed from the north. This Division was to come from their road construction duty detailed in Thailand.
4. The task of capturing Kohima was vested in the 31st Japanese Infantry Division under Kotoku Sato. This will proceed *via* Dimapur Imphal road.

Formation of the INA

On 7th December, 1941 Japanese aircraft struck the U.S naval base at Pearl Harbor, on the island of Hawaii causing great destruction and damage to American battleships, aircrafts and smaller vessels killing 2,403 people. With this, the hitherto simmering political situation in Europe overcast the clouds of World War II. The nations of the world split up into two opposing war camps — the USA, Great Britain, France, the USSR and China called the Allied on the one side and the Nazi Germany under Hitler, the Fascist Italy under Mussolini and Japan under Hirohito, called the Axis Power grouped on the other side. Soon the war spread like wild fire and engulfed as many as five continents of the world involving more than two-thirds of the world's population. The thunder and fury of war raged in Britain, Greece, Yugoslavia, Albania, Russia, Egypt, Iraq, Syria and Burma. The Japanese army landed in Malaya and penetrated across the Slim river zone held by the British army. Within a matter of hours the post held by Indian army was overrun by a massive force of fifty Japanese Tanks. The Indian forces had to retreat towards south to the fortress of Singapore to join the British India and Australian columns. The Japanese launched a series of attacks, first on the Australian column on 8/9 February, and then on the 11th Indian Division, by a force of 5,000 strong who infiltrated on the island under cover of darkness. (Peter Harclerode and David Reynolds — *Gurkha The Illustrated History*. 2003, Sutton Publishing Ltd. Gloucestershire, p. 42).

On 15th February, 1942 Singapore fell to the Japanese army and the next day the British army laid down their arms and surrendered at Singapore. On 17th February 4,500 Indian prisoners of war (POWs) were marched to a Farrer Park where Major Iwaichi Fujiwara, the Chief of Intelligence of the 15th Japanese army, addressed them telling them of the impending collapse of the British and the Allied forces and inviting them to join the INA for the liberation of India. Captain Mohan Singh, one of the Indian army officers who had surrendered to Japanese army earlier, in his address to the POWs explained the purpose for which the INA was formed and urged upon them to join hands in the noble cause of freeing Mother India. In the thick of the war the events moved so fast that the change of sides by the Indian POWs seemed to have taken place instantaneously and *en masse*. All the Indian army officers and the soldiers having accepted the call given by Captain Mohan Singh with enthusiasm and excitement, were handed over by Major Fujiwara to Captain Mohan Singh to form part of the INA. In such a dramatic turn of events the Gorkhas who were known for their discipline and loyalty to their master were in a state of psychological shock unable to make up their mind. But soon after they were separated from the British prisoners of war and put together with the Indian POWs, they were able to get over from the fear and confusion and to come to a common decision. The inspiring speeches of Captain Mohan Singh and Pritam Singh were now well received by the Gorkhas who raised their hands to show their willingness to join the INA. The first among the Gorkha soldiers to join the INA were, of course, the Indian born Gorkha officers who were later followed by other ranks including those coming from Nepal. Most of these pioneering Gorkha officers were the children of middle class Gorkha ex-servicemen who had settled down in various parts of India and became Indian citizens. They were settled in India for generations and had merged themselves into the Indian socio-cultural mainstream. Many of the Gorkha POWs hailed from places like Dharamsala, Dehra-Dun, Almorah, Nainital, etc., and were bred in Indian environ. To cite a few instances, Captain Sher Bahadur Bhandari of 2/9 Gorkha Rifles and Naik Dhan Bahadur Gurung, 2/2 GR hailed from Dehra-Dun; Captain Bhimsingh Thapa, 2/1 GR and Lance Naik Bahadur Singh, 2/9 GR. were from Almorah. All these Gorkha soldiers together with many other Gorkhas joined the INA and laid down their lives for the cause of India's freedom.

Subhas Chandra Bose took over the leadership of the INA which was christened as 'Azad Hind Fauz', on 4th July, 1943 at Singapore. In a series of meetings between the INA leaders and the Japanese it was decided to cede of the IIL (Indian Independence League) and the INA to Subhas Bose since majority of the Indian prisoners of war expressed their opinion that they were willing to join the INA only on the condition that it was led by Subhas Chandra Bose. Immediately after assuming the charge, Bose reorganised the fledging INA which previously consisted of only the POWs by enlisting the support of the Indian expatriates in South Asia as local civilians ranging from traders, plantation workers, shop-keepers who had no military experience. They all came voluntarily to join the INA. Thus, the INA was composed of (1) the POWs captured at Singapore, (2) Indian soldiers numbering 3,500, captured earlier in the west and recruited from European and African prison camps originally called Indian Legion, (3) Indian soldiers captured in previous battles from Malayaan Peninsula which were inspired by Rash Behari Bose to fight against British and formed into an organization called `The Indian Independence League' and (4) the civilian Indian population of South Asia.

The INA (Azad Hind Fauz) under Subhas Bose was divided into three broad divisions and placed under the following officers:

1. The 1st Division was under Mohammad Zaman Kiyani which consisted of the following regiments:

    - The Second Guerrilla regiment or the Gandhi Brigade with two infantry battalions.
    - The 3rd Guerrilla regiment or Azad Brigade consisting of three battalions.
    - The 4th Guerrilla regiment or the Nehru Brigade under Lt. Col. G.S. Dhillon.

- The 1st Guerrilla regiment or the Subhas Brigade under Col. Shah Nawaz Khan with three infantry battalions.

2. The Second Division was under Aziz Ahmad and consisted of:
   * The 1st Infantry Regiment, later to be merged with the 5th Guerrilla regiment to form part of 2nd Infantry regiment.
   * The 5th Guerrilla regiment to be renamed as 2nd Infantry regiment.
   * The Rani of Jhansi regiment composed of female volunteers from Malaya and Burma under Lakshmi Sahgal.
3. The 3rd Division of the INA was composed of the local volunteers of Singapore and Malaya. This was disbanded before Japan surrendered.

One of the most striking features of the INA which distinguished it from the British Indian Army was that there was complete unity and solidarity among the INA jawans transcending all barriers of caste, community and religion. Their leader "Netaji" was the fountain-head of all power and inspiration and the symbol of unity among the Hindu, Muslim Sikh and others. There was no distinction between any culture, caste and creed. They lived under the same roof, shared the same food and aimed at one objective, i.e., to free their motherland from the foreign yoke. During those days, when in India Hindu and Muslim relations posed the greatest challenge to Indian political leaders and took away much of the required wind out of the sail of Indian National Congress, the INA held out a unique example of unity in diversity. Mahatma Gandhi who could never reconcile himself with the idea of using violence for India's freedom admittedly remarked — "Though the INA failed in their immediate objective they have a lot to their credit of which they might well be proud. Great among them was to gather together under one banner men from all religions and races of India and to infuse into them the spirit of solidarity and oneness to the utter exclusion of all communal or political sentiment. It is an example which we should amulate". (*Harijan* : April 14, 1946)

Undoubtedly, this spirit of absolute oneness in religion and in purpose was infused by the charismatic leadership of their firebrand leader, Subhas Chandra Bose. In his historic call to his jawans, in particular and the Indians in general, he said — "Give me your blood and I shall give you freedom". He introduced heart boiling slogans like — "Delhi Chalo" and "Jai Hind", of which the latter slogan has been adopted by the Government of India. The INA's marching song—*"Kadam, kadam badhaey ja, khusi ke geet gaey ja"* which was composed and tuned by Ramsingh Thakuri, a Gorkha Bandmaster of the INA has become very popular even among the Indian civil population. He also rendered the poem — *"Jana Gana Mana"*, composed by poet Ravindranath Tagore, into martial tune and orchestrated it in full military band, for the first time, on October 21, 1943 before a largely attended ceremony held at Darbar Hall of the Cathay building at Singapore on the occasion of the formation of the Azad Hind Government. Subhas Bose loved this song to the core of his heart and adopted it as INA song. After India became independent the song has been adopted as its National Anthem.

Indian Gorkhas : Their Socio-Political Background

A glimpse into the socio-political history of the Indian Gorkhas residing in India reveals that they have not only become socially and culturally merged with their Indian neighbours but also were politically conscious ever since the first quarter of the twentieth century. The Indian Gorkhas living in northern India like Delhi, Dehra-Dun, Nainital, Almorah, etc., were politically influenced by the nationalist leaders of India and actively participated in various political movements related to India's freedom. They were closely involved in the Arya Samaj movement led by Swami Dayananda Saraswati whose doctrine of *'Swaraja, Swabhasa, Swadharma'* attracted the Gorkhas. Through this organisation they came under the influence of great national leaders like Lala Lajpat Rai who initially showed the seed of nationalism among the Gorkhas of these places. They also took part in Civil Disobedience movement led by Mahatma Gandhi and later on in the 'Quit India' movement of 1942 and many of them suffered imprisonment. Places like Dehra-Dun, Nainital, Almorah being the part of Nepalese territory till the treaty of Sigouly (1815) these areas were home to a good number of original Nepalese from Terai, besides the ex-servicemen of British creation. In 1930s when the Civil Disobedience movement launched by Mahatma Gandhi swept the country, the Gorkhas of Dehra-Dun, Nalapani and Delhi rose to the occasion and rallied under the banner of Indian National Congress. Gorkha leaders like Dhruba Singh Thapa, Ritha Singh, Hukum Singh, Dal Bahadur Thapa, Lal Bir Newar, etc., together with Gorkha men and women held picketing and courted arrest

The INA roll also included a good number of Gorkha soldiers from the district of Darjeeling as well as the hills and plains of undivided Assam who were equally conscious in nationalist movement. The Gorkhas of Darjeeling being socially, culturally and politically more advanced, they had been in the forefront among the other Nepalis living in India. Their involvement in the national political movement can be traced back to the year 1921 when a host of Gorkhas from Darjeeling, Kalimpong and Kurseong took part in the non-co-operation movement and suffered imprisonment. Shaheed Bhagatvir Tamang was the first ever Gorkha martyr of the Indian freedom struggle. Similarly, in Assam the names of Babu Chabilal Upadhyaya, Hari Prasad Upadhyaya, Bhakta Bahadur Pradhan, Dalvir Singh Lohar and Bishnulal Upadhyaya, etc., have all passed into the recorded history of India's freedom movement. This was the kind political background of the places from where the Gorkha soldiers were drawn into the INA who had fought against the British in Burma, Imphal and Kohima and laid down their lives.

It is, therefore, wrong to presume that the Gorkha soldiers who took part in the war against British in the World War II as part of the INA were not inspired by nationalist ideas as some historians seem to have maintained. I have chosen to discuss this aspect of the INA Gorkhas purposely in order to correct the views of some gullible Indian academics who tend to believe that the Gorkhas joined the INA not really being inspired by the spirit of nationalism like those Indian soldiers but under the pressure and compelling situation. This view is misleading and is as much incorrect as to say that the Gorkhas did not join the INA at all, as some English writers have stated. The Britishers had a deep seated belief in their mind that the naive Gorkhas could not have changed side like Indian soldiers since they had been found loyal, obedient and straightforward all through and had served the British well ever since their recruitment in Indian army. The Gorkhas may be naive and simple but when it comes to the question of motherland they cannot compromise their love for her, for anything else, because, these Gorkha soldiers who joined the INA were born and brought up on Indian soil and held India as their home and motherland. The trial and passing the death sentences upon the two Gorkha INA soldiers, *viz.*, Major Durga Malla and Captain Dal Bahadur Thapa by the Court Martial held in Delhi in 1944 stand out as the decisive proof of the fact that the Gorkha boys had joined the INA and fought against the British army with the intention of liberating India being fully inspired by the fire of Indian nationalism. The Court Martial that was constituted for the trial and disposal of cases of the INA soldiers captured by British Indian army had set forth certain principles for the purpose of awarding punishment on the basis of the degree and severity of the offences committed by each INA soldier. According to this principle the offenders were broadly grouped into four categories—1. Those who joined the INA with the intention of deserting or sabotaging it would be classed as 'white' and they would be aacquitted and restored to their previous poisitions; 2. those who yielded to the pressure and joined the INA would be classed as 'Grey' and would be treated with mercy and generosity. They would be summarily tried, dismissed and released; 3. those who joined the INA willingly would be classified as 'Black'. They would be tried, dismissed and in most cases their penalty would be commuted for short period imprisonment; and 4. the most serious offences would be those who held responsible positions previously and later on joined the INA willingly with an intention to overthrow the British Government and committed atrocities to forces to join the INA. They would be classed as the 'Blackest' and would be charged for the offence of waging a war against the British Government and would be sentenced to be hanged until death. It is apparent from the above criteria of punishment adopted by the Court Martial that the two Gorkha INA jawans were judged as those offenders who joined the INA willingly with an intention to wage a war to overthrow the British Government and were classed as the 'Blackest' and were awarded the severest punishment of death by hanging. The above fact of finding the nature of offences and awarding of death sentences to Major Durga Malla and Captain

Dal Bahadur Thapa by the Court Martial goes to prove without doubt that the Gorkha soldiers who had joined the INA willingly and fought against the British for the liberation of India were the true sons of Indian soil who laid down their lives for their motherland. They were not the only INA Gorkhas who made supreme sacrifice of lives for the country — there were as many as twenty-two others who joined the INA and got killed in the war as named by Dr. P.N.Chopra in his book, *'Who is Who of Indian Martyrs'* Vol., I. 1969. The names and details about these twenty-four INA Gorkhas have been given at the Appendix, as they could not be accommodated here due to space constraints.

At the small hours of 25th August, 1944 Major Durga Malla was led to the gallows in Delhi and hanged until death. The historic spot where Shaheed Durga Malla was hanged to death is situated within the Maulana Azad Medical College compound, New Delhi and it is named Shaheed Park. To commemorate this day of 25th August the Gorkhas in India observe *'Balidan Diwas'* (Martyr Day) and pay tributes to the soul of this great martyr at this auspicious place every year. The Bharatiya Gorkha Parisangh, the only representative body of Indian Nepalis, raised a statue of Shaheed Durga Malla within the premises of the Parliament House, New Delhi. This status was ceremonially unveiled by Dr. Manmohan Singh, the former Prime Minister of India on 17 December, 2004, in a largely attended function in the presence of Bhairon Singh Shekhawat, the Vice President of India; Sonia Gandhi, All India Congress President; Somnath Chatterjee, Speaker of Lok Sabha; L.K. Advani, Leader of Opposition; Shivnath Patil, Home Minister and Pranab Mukherjee, the then Defence Minister of India. The 18 feet high statue of bronze was sculpted by renowned sculptor, Gautam Pal of Kolkata which depicts Shaheed Durga Malla seated on a galloping horse with a bare *khukhri* in hand. Thus, shaheed Durga Malla has been remembered by the nation for his supreme sacrifice and I extend my deep gratitude to the Bharatiya Gorkha Parisangh for this commendable task, but unfortunately Captain Dal Bahadur Thapa who was also captured by British army as INA soldier and hanged to death on the 3rd May, 1945 in Delhi, according to Dr. P.N. Chopra, has not been accorded the same honour till today. I urge upon the Bharatiya Gorkha Parisangh and the leaders among Indian Nepalis at large to take steps to research into the history about this great martyr and give him his due share of honour as has been done to Shaheed Durga Malla. It is also, incumbent upon the Nepali scholars and academics of India, as a whole, to conduct research works on the role played by the Gorkhas and the trial of INA soldiers by British Court Martial in New Delhi, since many aspects still remain in the dark about the facts and circumstance as to how the three top Indian INA leaders viz., Col. G.S. Dhillon, Col. Shah Nawaz Khan and Captain P.K. Sehgal who were also captured by British and charged for same offences of treason and waging war against British Government were, ultimately, set free while the two petty Gorkha INA soldiers were executed. Was it that General Claude Auchinleck, the Commander-in-Chief of British Indian Army did not find sufficient evidence against them or was he influenced by extrajudicial considerations at the behest of the Indian National Congress is a matter to be brought to light.

The INA Gorkhas in Operation

In the INA the Gorkha soldiers played a crucial role with their classic fighting spirit, grit and courage in every front and every military action. Their physical hardiness and climatic endurance helped them to push forward through the thick jungles and the mountain fastness of Burma. Their versatility in the technique of guerrilla fighting added extra capability to the Gorkha which was appreciated by Netaji. This apart, similiarity of their appearance with the local inhabitants of Burma proved to be of special advantage to the Gorkhas which they could profitably utilize in their duty of espionage. The Gorkha officers with their matured experience and drill-book discipline were considered to be fit for imparting training to INA new recruits in the art of jungle combat and guerrilla warfare. There were altogether sixteen military training centres run by the INA at different places including one Gorkha training school at Kamba in Rangoon. Besides normal fighting against the enemy the Gorkha soldiers also carried out reconnaissance and intelligence duties. This job involved grave danger for life and required immense courage and tactfulness. It was in this particular task that the Gorkhas could make use of their Mongolian look with advantage as they looked similar in disguise with the civilian hill tribes of the place and they could freely mix up and make friends with them and sneak out valuable information about the enemy plan and positions. Sometimes they were caught by the enemy and killed. One Gorkha soldier named Bhupal Singh was captured by the British troops while performing intelligence duty in the Arakan and was killed. He belonged to 2/5 Gorkha Rifles and had joined the INA in 1942 at Singapore.

Launching of anti-British propaganda and carrying out subversive activities through specially trained men was one of the most important war strategies of Subhas Bose. This programme consisted of disseminating messages and appeals through the radio and printed materials in vernacular among the British Indian soldiers and sometimes even by personal contacts and to instigate them not to fight for the foreign ruler but to join INA in order to liberate India from the colonial power. The Gorkha soldiers played a significant role in this programme as evidenced from the following extract taken from the Survey Report on the activities of the INA dated 17 April, 1943. (IORF. No.L/WS/1/1576)

> "Recent information shows that a Gorkha O.R. (other rank) who was taken prisoner during the Burma campaign early in 1942 and was in Japanese hands for over six months, volunteered for 'contact work' in Burma in the course of which he rejoined our forces at Magwe with other fifth-column volunteers. Subsequently, he deserted taking with him a Jamadar and two G.O.R.s (Gorkha other ranks) fifth column companion. He then surrendered to Japanese and again joined the fifth-column party at Yanangyung and accompanied it to Mandalaya and Myomo. Later he returned to Rangoon where he was detailed to form one of the fifth-column parties which left for India at the end of August 1942 with instructions to collaborate with Congress workers and help them in destroying communications, dumps, etc.
>
> Incidentally, although most of the responsibilities involved in this episode were Gurkhas this does not indicate the conclusion reached in paragraph 3 of Survey Report No. 13 of 1943 where the reaction of Gurkha to INA propaganda were discussed. It is perhaps, significant that neither the Gurkha O.R., the

> successful propagandist accompanied him nor any of the soldiers who were reduced from their loyalty in this affair, came from Nepal. The two Japanese agents are line boys from Almorah and Dharamshala respectively. The Jamadar is also a Dharamshala line boy while one of the O.R. is a Darjeeling Gurkha."

The above Survey Report which emanated from a source no other than the General Headquarters of the British Indian army is an irrefutable testimony to the important role played by the Gorkha soldiers in the INA. The Report is also explicit about the secret nexus established between the INA Gorkha fifth columnists and the Revolutionary wing of the Congress and the Forward Bloc that were active within the Indian mainland for carrying out subversive acts of disrupting the British war efforts in which the Gorkha INA activists took a very significant role. The following extract taken from Leonard A. Cordon's book entitled *Brothers Against Raj* will reveal about the secret communication link that existed between Subhas Bose and his men in the midland India and how the Gorkha INA men maintained secret link forming small groups equipped with wireless.

> "It may be noted how the B.V. arose out of the 1928 Calcutta Congress and how they remained devoted to Bose through the 1939s. With the war's outbreak and then Bose's escape the group remained ready to carry out the orders. When Bose in Berlin communicated either through Bhagat Ram in Kabul or through Japanese channel to Sarat Bose in Calcutta instructions were passed on to B.V. through Bakshi. Then B.V. men tried to send operatives across the frontiers to Burma in 1943 and 1944 and Bose, with Japanese assistance tried to send small groups of men equipped with wireless into India. Most of these groups were caught, some imprisoned and few executed". (Leonard A. Gordon — *Brothers Against Raj*, New Delhi, 1990, pp. 476-77)

Needless to say that such a duty of espionage really involved great risks which called for skill, tactfulness and immense courage. But the Gorkha boys could manage to do it successfully to the satisfaction of their officers. They were clever, intelligent and trained enough to plan their strategies as per the prevailing conditions which was the secret of their success. For according to the survey Report referred to above the INA fifth column volunteers who carried out their tasks successfully were not from Nepal but from India only. Two of them including the Jamadar were line boys from Dharamshala, one from Almorah and one from Darjeeling. Disguised as belonging to the Gorkha Rifles of the Indian Army with torn and worn out uniforms on their bodies they pretended as having been captured by the Japanese and subsequently escaped from their prison these fifth-columnists succeeded to get themselves readmitted in the Indian army. Then they instigated against the British rule and induced the Gorkha soldiers to run away and join the INA. In this way there were many such fifth-column parties in Burma where the Gorkha INA agents carried out 'Contact works' and coaxed away Indian Gorkha soldiers from British camps. Obviously the kind of job needed tremendons courage and factfulness which was possible only for the Indian Gorkhas.

K.S. Giani in his book entitled Indian Independence Movement in East Asia 1947, Lahore, gives a classic example of such contact work of a Gorkha INA officer as follows :

> "As the war was blazing in the Arakan hills an order was issued from INA Headquarters that one should immediately be deputed for anti British propaganda work in the enemy camp on the other side of the hillock. Lieutenant Durga Bahadur volunteered himself for this mission. He disguised himself as a Gorkha officer of the Indian army and crossed over to the enemy post risking his life. There he made personal contacts with the Gorkha soldiers, held secret talks, passed on the bundles of INA pamphlets and returned back successfully to his camp the next morning. Lieutenant Durga Bahadur was awarded *"Sanad E-Bahadur'* by Netaji for his gallant enterprise in March 1944".

The Gorkhas were frequently engaged in the espionage and

subversive works like this who penetrated deep into the Indian army camps and distributed leaflets and propaganda materials issued from the INA Headquarters. The following letter issued from the General Head Office of the British Indian Army to the G.O.C. of Indian Army (File No. 601/1C-469-H Army Deptt.) dated 18 March, 1943 stands as documentary evidence of the act of extreme risk and responsibility undertaken by the Gorkha boys for the INA.

> "In a disquieting number of cases individuals have managed to conceal from interrogation the fact that they have been in Japanese hands ; have been coached in espionage and subversive propaganda and sent back with specific instructions. Cases are now coming to light of stragglers who rejoined as long ago as August and September and have successfully concealed these facts. In spite of instruction issued under A.G. Branch 30065/AG-22 of 27-7-42, in some cases such men have been reposted to unit in Eastern Army or having joined then direct have been allowed to remain there. Japanese are now reinforcing "deep penetration" agents with leaflets and radio propaganda addressed directly to Indian troops and issued in the name of INA. Manuscript letters in vernacular script and emanating from Captain Mohan Singh have been picked up by our patrol in Arakan."

The war between the INA and the British Indian army was, indeed, a unique battle ever fought in the history of India — a battle where the Indian fought against Indian, Sikh against the Sikh, Rajput against Rajput and the Gorkha against Gorkha. The brother fought against brother and killed each other, knowingly or unknowingly. It may so happen that they were in the same regiment or battalion while in the Indian army. Many Gorkha soldiers of the Indian army got killed by the Gorkhas in the INA and many of them acquitted themselves well in the battle and earned Victoria Crosses in Arakan hills.

As the Japanese army opened offensive, the INA also sent its forces into battle. The INA's strategy was, of course to avoid set-piece battle as they lacked sufficient arms for such offensive. However, Netaji Subhas Bose had made it clear to General Kawabe, the Japanese Commander in Burma, that his INA would be the spearhead of the whole operation as soon as it penetrates into India. He wanted that the first drop of blood to be shed on the Indian soil would be that of a member of the INA. Once the Japanese forces were able to break the British defence at Imphal the INA would cross the hills of North East India into the Gangetic plain where it would work as a guerrilla force in collaboration with local Indians for freeing India. Prem Kumar Sahgal, an officer of INA and once secretary to Subhas Bose stated that once the INA got into the Gangetic plain, even if the Japanese lost the war the Britain would not be able to assert its colonial authority which was the ultimate aim of the INA and the Azad Hind Fouz. Accordingly, due role was given to INA to play in the operation which started on the 15th March, 1944.

As the Japanese attack on India began, the INA's first Division consisting of four Guerrilla regiments took the lead in operation. A Bahadur group unit led by Saukat Malik took the border enclave of Moirang in early April while the main body of the first Division marched ahead successfully. The initial success of the INA at the Arakan front generated much enthusiasm among the troops. In a special order of the day Netaji referred to the "glorious and brilliant action of the brave soldiers of Azad Hind Fauz". The INA fighting side by side with Japanese troops crossed the Burma border and set their feet on the soil of India near Kohima which fell to them on 6th April, 1944. However by the time Khan's reinforcement column left Tamu and reached Ukhrul, in the vicinity of Kohima their offensive had been held by British forces. The other columns proceeding to Imphal suffered the same fate. The 33 Division of Japanese army fought desperately for forty days without being able to penetrate the British lines near Imphal. Finally on 5 July, 1944 the Japanese General Mutaguchi ordered to halt the operation and the Japanese troops started withdrawal. With little or no supplies and replenishment of supply being hampered by heavy monsoon the INA could not hold on any more. The Gorkhas in their effort to live up to the high ideals of their great leader Netaji, displayed extreme bravery and laid down their lives in hundreds.

The following account recorded by the Intelligence Department of the Government of India stands for it:

> "A measure of courage cannot be denied to the leaders of INA front-line units in Burma in 1945 when they faced up to British equipment, tanks, guns and aircraft with rifles and bullock carts and empty stomach."

As the withdrawal of Japanese troops progressed and the provision of foodstuff exhausted the INA soldiers had to withdraw following the Japanese. The Japanese proved themselves to be reckless adventurous to carry an absolute minimum of supplies hoping that they would overrun British troops and capture enemy supplies which did not happen at all. When shortage of ration really hit them they were loath to share the residue with the INA troops. Shah Nawaz who led the INA troops recounts that his men had to subsist on jungle foods and that about seventy per cent of them were stricken with illness as medicines ran out and many men died of hunger and illness. He bitterly wrote:

> "With clear conscience I can say that the Japanese did not give full aid and assistance to the Azad Hind Fouz during their assault on Imphal they let us down badly and had it not been for their betrayal of the INA the history of the Imphal campaign might have been different one. The Japanese did not trust the INA. They had found out through their Liaison Officer that the INA would not accept Japanese domination in any way and that they would fight the Japanese in case they attempted to replace the British..............They were too confident of themselves and thought that they would be able to capture Imphal without assistance and without much difficulty." (Shah Nawaz Khan, *My Memories of INA*, Delhi, 1946, p. 126) .

During their hasty retreat into Burma the INA soldiers suffered terrible fate ; as wounded, starved and diseased men many of them succumbed to death. The withdrawing forces suffered casualties from allied airplanes strafing them and the Chinese guerrillas harassed the Japanese troops. The story of retreat from Imphal was one of the greatest tragedies of the World War II. It is a story of hunger, thirst, disease and death. According to an estimate out of 220,000 Japanese troops only 130,000 survived and of these only 70,000 remained at the front to retreat. The INA casualties were more than fifty per cent of their strength. A large number of INA troops surrendered to British army under Lt.Col. Loganathan while the remaining troops retreated with Subhas Bose towards Malaya. Netaji Subhas Chandra Bose accepted the defeat with the large heart and complimented his officers and brave soldiers in the following words :

> "We started the operation too late. The monsoon was disadvantageous to us...... In the Kaladan sector we routed the enemy and advanced. In Tiddim we advanced, in Palel and Kohima also we advanced. In Haka sector we held them. And all this, in spite of numerical superiority that the enemy had, plus equipment and rations ..... We have received our baptism of fire, our troops have gained much confidence".(Subhas Bose — *Selected Speeches*, pp. 219-20)

The unfortunate turn of events in the war prevented Netaji's dream of victorious march to Delhi from becoming a reality. Netaji Subhas Chandra Bose, the greatest patriot and India's freedom fighter is presumed to have died on 18 August, 1945 in a plane crash while flying to Tokyo, although a contradictory view is also taken by some people. With his sudden demise the INA's war of India's liberation ended in failure but the daunted efforts and supreme sacrifice made by the Indian soldiers of the INA will ever be remembered by Indians with deep gratitude. The following few anecdotes about the bravery, doggedness and sacrifices made by the Gorkha INA soldiers will remain for ever written in golden letters.

One Kalu Singh Lama fought as a last man to the last round

and shed his blood on the bank of river Chindwin. On the morning of 31 December, 1943 a column of motorized enemy troops advanced towards his position. Kalu Lama and his men put up a stubborn resistance with their old rifles which were no match to enemy's heavy artilleries. He tried to hold his position fighting courageously until their ammunitions exhausted and he, along with his men, were pinned down by enemy shelling. Another Manilal Gurung who joined the Bahadur Group of the INA came under a massive attack on his march towards Imphal in the Indo-Burma border. He fought bravely holding his position without letting the enemy to advance forward while he was hit on the chest by a bullet and fell dead on the spot. One Sital Bahadur of the 1st Bahadur Battalion of the INA met with the same fate near Ramokori (Burma) in August 1844 after a hand to hand fight against the enemy. On another occasion Second Lieutenant Gyansing Bist was leading his company of 98 strong near Indo-Burma border on the morning of 16th March, 1945 when a column of motorized troops consisting of several tanks, armoured jeeps and trucks advanced towards them. They had no machinegun or even a light machine-gun except the good old rifles to fight with. Gyansingh and his men did not lose heart; they waited in their position until the steel monsters approached close to them creating hell with their fire power when Lt. Bist leading the assault shouted — *'Inqilab jindabad, Netaji ki Jai'*. His men quickly responded with their guns and there ensued a gun battle which lasted for half an hour when most of his men fell on the ground. But Gyansingh would not give in. He jumped upon the enemy *with glittering khukuri in hand followed by* his men and engaged in hand to hand fight chopping the heads of enemies until he fell to the bullet of the enemy never to give out command any more.

Some fortunate INA Gorkhas survived the onslaught of the war and returned back home to recount their chequered experience to people around them. One such person was Nar Bahadur Gurung of Shillong (Meghalaya) who joined the INA together with his fellow Gorkha soldiers in 1942. Earlier he was a soldier in the 4/8 Gorkha Rifles and was taken prisoner of war by the Japanese at Singapore. During the INA operation he was captured by the British Indian army at Kohima border in 1944 and imprisoned in Delhi jail. After independence he was released from the jail along with many others with a certificate of commendation from the Prime Minister, Jawaharlal Nehru. He was readmitted in 1/8 Gorkha Rifles till his retirement. In 1998 he was honoured as a freedom fighter and presented with a shawl and a plaque by the Subhas Chandra Bose Centenary Celebration Committee of Shillong.

Repatriation and Trial

After the end of the war a large number of INA soldiers surrendered to the British Indian army who were estimated to be 16,000. There were also many who were captured earlier during the operation at Imphal and on their subsequent withdrawal among the hills of Arakan. A small number of them had also fallen into the Allied hands in 1943 around the time of Kohima campaign. The majority of these captured INAs had been shipped back to India by July 1945 Those repatriated were passed through transit camps in Chittagong and Calcutta to be held at detention camps located at various places in India including Jhingergacha, Nilganj, near Calcutta, Kirkee outside Pune, Attock, Multan and Bahadurgarh near Delhi. These surrendered and captured INAs were interrogated, scrutinized and classified according to their degree of offences on the basis of the criteria adopted by British Army administration. According to the criteria they designated the captured troops into four categories. Those who joined the INA without any commitment to Azad Hind, as 'Whites', They were restored to their previous posts. Those who believed and merely followed their fellow INA as 'Greys' — they were released from imprisonment without punishment. Those who joined INA willingly as 'Blacks' — they were tried and dismissed and those who joined INA willingly with the intention to overthrow the British Government as the 'Blackests'— they were tried and sentenced to death. All the captured and surrendered INAs were interrogated and tried and punished according to their offences as mentioned above. Major Durga Malla and Captain Dal Bahadur Thapa were sentenced to death and executed. Major Puran Singh Thakur was sentenced to seven years imprisonment, Colonel Dilman Singh Thapa, Captain Ram Singh Thakur, Chandrabir Gurung, Man Bahadur Rai, Asman Singh Pradhan, Rup Narayan Pradhan, Buddha Singh Gurung, Ram Singh Basnet and many others were dismissed from their services. (B.L. Upadhyaya — Khan Mihali, 2004, p.33) No one was sentenced to death except the two unfortunate Gorkhas Durga Malla and Dal Bahadur Thapa as mentioned in the preceding paragraphs. Not even the most celebrated leaders of the INA like Clolonel Prem Sehgal, Colonel Gurubaksh Singh Dhillon, and Major Shah Nawaz Khan who were categorized as the 'Blackest' offenders were executed. Their trials were held at the Red Fort, Delhi by the Army Court Martial and were found guilty of waging war against the King of England and Emperor of British India and were sentenced to imprisonment for life. Their trial generated much interest and public sympathy for the INA leaders who were perceived as the real patriots of India. The Indian National Congress rose to the occasion and legal luminaries in the person of Jawaharlal Nehru, Bhulabhai Desai, Kailashnath Katju came forward to defend the INA leaders in the Court Martial. Muslim League also joined hand with the Congress and sent reputed lawyer like Asaf Ali to plead for them. The release of the three defendants was made a political issue and tagged together with the movement for freedom in 1945-46. Public demonstrations were held demanding dismissal of the cases and unconditional release of the INA leaders. General Auchinleck, the Commander-in-Chief of Indian Army was ultimately compelled to go by the recommendation of Lord Mount Batten and stop implementation of the sentence pronounced by the Court Martial against the three INA leaders. The lives of the three INA leaders were saved. Nehru later remarked — "It became a trial of strength between the will of the Indian people and the will of those who held power in *India, and it was the will of the people that triumphed in the end"*.

The Impact of INA War

From the military point of view the INA's impact on the war, as a whole, can be termed as insignificant, given its small numerical strength and the absence of heavy and effective weaponry. With the old and outdated British arms captured with the Indian soldiers, the INA may be said to have played the second fiddle in actual fight while on the war front. But it must be accepted that its jawans played a crucial role in the final assault on Imphal and Kohima as well as during their withdrawal through Manipur and Burma.

Earlier while still under Mohan Singh's command its special group carried out significant work in halting the first Arakan offensive. Their Commanding Officer, Shah Nawaz Khan, in his personal memoirs claimed that the INA was a very potent and motivated force. In espionage and anti-British propaganda work the INA boys discharged very commendable duties. Launching propaganda and subversive activity through a specially trained INA men was one of the most important war strategies of Subhas Bose. We have discussed in the preceding paragraphs how the Gorkha INAs, in complete disregard of their life's danger, penetrated into the enemy camps in disguise of local tribals and distributed propaganda materials among the Indian troops to destroy their loyalty in the British Government. The potentiality of threat posed to the Allied forces by the daring acts of espionage carried out by the Gorkha special group can be very well imagined from the reports emanated from the British army Headquarters. The principal objective of the INA was to liberate India from British occupation with Japanese assistance which could not be done because of various reasons beyond the command and capability of the INA.

Thus, the INA failed to liberate India but, indirectly, it had a far reaching effect on the British policy of colonial rule in India which, in the long run, contributed to the accelerated achievement of independence to India. The civil disobedience and non-violence movement launched by Mahatma Gandhi, left to itself, would not have brought freedom to India so soon as it came in 1947, immediately after the close of the second World War. It was the cumulative effect of the armed revolution of the INA, the Sepoy Mutiny (War of Independence) of 1857 and the Quit India Movement of 1942 which combined together to drive the British Government to seriously think over the future of India. In the words of Michael Edward, the British historian in his — *Last Years of British India* :

> "The fact that Government of India's own army men captured in Burma by Japanese changed sides against the British Government made the Government of India realize that the Indian army, its sole strength, might now no longer be trustworthy."

The Sepoy Mutiny of 1857, the rebellion of Royal Indian Navy of 1946 and the change of allegiance by the captured soldiers of Indian army in 1942 acted as the potential reminders to the British Parliament to rethink about the future political relations with the people of India. Mr. Attlee, the Prime Minister of Great Britain himself had very well realized the situation when he said:

> "Among the principal reasons the one was the erosion of loyalty to British Crown among the Indian Army and Navy personnel as a result of military activities of Netaji."

After the conclusion of the World War II in 1945 the captured and surrendered INA men were brought to Delhi and put on trial by Court Martial on charges of treason and waging war against the Government of British India. Many prisoners were sentenced to death penalty, life imprisonment and fine or imprisonment. In between November 1945 and May 1946 as many as ten Court Martials were held and the top INA leaders like P.K. Sehgal, G.S. Dhillon and Shah Nawaz Khan whose names had already become popular among the people of India were sentenced to life imprisonment. These trials and heavy punishments imposed on these freedom fighters generated wide publicity and public sympathy among mass people who organized public demonstration demanding their unconditional release. This was another reason that came up for consideration of the British Parliament in regard to India's future policy. Ramesh Chandra Majumdar, an eminemt historian observed in his book — *Three Phases of India's Struggle for Freedom*, Bombay, 1967, pp. 58-59.

> "The battle for India's freedom were also being fought against Britain, though indirectly, by Hitler in Europe and Japan in Asia. None of these scored direct success, but few would deny that it was the cumulative effect of all three that brought freedom to India. In particular, the revelations made by INA trial and the reaction it produced in India made it quite plain to the British, already exhausted by the

> war, that they would no longer depend upon the loyalty of these sepoys for maintaining their authority in India. This had probably, the greatest influence upon their final decision to quit India."

It will, thus be wrong to say that the war of the INA (Azad Hind Fouz) ended in fiasco without yielding any result. *But the supreme sacrifice made by the gallant sons of India went a long way to accelerate the process for achieving India's independence and for this, we the future generations must feel proud of them and remember them for ever.* Unfortunately, very few Indians seem to know about them today nor any stone is raised to commemorate their supreme sacrifice. On the other hand, far away from India, at Singapore, there stands a monument that was erected by Netaji Subhas Chandra Bose himself immediately after the war, which proclaims the heroic deeds and supreme sacrifices of the INA soldiers and pays rich tributes to them all. It reads :

> "Future generations of Indians who will be born, not as slaves but as free man, because of your colossal sacrifice, will bless your names and proudly proclaim to the world that you, their forebears, fought and suffered reverses in the battles in Manipur, Assam and Burma, but through temporary failure you paved the way to ultimate success and glory."
>
> To commemorate Netaji Subhas Chandra Bose the following words have been inscribed on the brass shield in front of the chair on which Subhas Chandra Bose used to sit in his office of the Azad Hind Government at Rangoon as a symbol of sovereign India.

"Netaji Subhas Chandra Bose in order to free India from the shackles of British imperialism organized the Azad Hind Government from outside the country on October 21, 1943. Netaji set up the provisional Government of Independent India (Azad Hind) and transferred its Headquarters at Rangoon on January 7, 1944. On the 5th April, 1944 the Azad Hind Bank was inaugurated at Rangoon. It was on this occasion that Netaji used this chair for the first time. Later the chair was kept at the residence of Netaji at 51, University Avenue, Rangoon, where the office of the Azad Hind is also housed. Afterwards, at the time of leaving Burma, the Britishers handed over the chair to the family of Mr. A.T.Ahuja, the well known businessman of Rangoon. The chair was officially handed over to the Government of India in January 1979. It was brought to Calcutta on the 17th July, 1980. It has now been ceremonially installed at the Red Fort on July 7, 1981."

6

Shaheed Durga Malla

Man is a queer homosapien. He is capable of martyrdom. Human history is replete with instances in which men have laid down their lives for the sake of noble causes. Defending one's own country from foreign invasion or liberating it from other's possession are the two most sacred grounds for which one is often prompted to die. They are indeed, the brave people who offer to do so. The Gorkhas belong to martial race and they are traditionally associated with warfare because they are capable of dying in battle. The Gorkha Rifles's motto is – "It is better to die than to be a coward". They are said to be the "bravest of the braves, most generous of the generous"(Ralf Turner). Thousands of Gorkhas have laid down their lives during the first and the second World Wars. They have left their dead in France, Gallipoli, the Suez and Mesopotamia. They have distinguished themselves in Burma, Malaya and Kohima for their bravery, tenacity and èlan. In the following paragraphs we shall discuss about one such brave Gorkha who fought against the British Indian army for liberation of India from the shackles of the British and sacrificed his precious life. The blessed name of this brave son of India is – Major Durga Bahadur Malla.

Birth and Childhood

Durga Malla was born on 1 July, 1913 at village Doiwala in the district of Dehra-Dun of Uttaranchal State. He was the eldest among the seven siblings of whom four were brothers and three sisters. Their father Gangaram Malla was an ex-serviceman who served as Naib-Subedar in the Gorkha Rifles and the mother Parwati was a house-wife. Gangaram's family lived a simple life with his meagre pension and petty source of income from agricultural pursuits. Growing of sugarcane crop, preparing molasses (gur) and selling in the market constituted their main profession. The land for agriculture, the main stay of Gangaram Malla, was inherited by him from his forefathers who had settled down in Doiwala ever since eighteenth century. Getting enlisted in the army and doing soldiery was their ancestral profession. In fact, the Gorkhas living in Dehradun, Nainital, Almorah, Dharamsala, etc., traditionally took to soldiery ever since the inception of the Gorkha Rifles. It was the Gorkha recruits from Dehradun, Nahan and Sirmoor who constituted the 4500 strong first Battalion of the Gorkha Rifles when Lieutenant Frederick Young raised it in 1815, before the Treaty of Sigauli was formally concluded.

Since his childhood Durga Malla was a hard working boy. He used to walk several miles every day to go to his school which was situated at a far distance from his paternal uncle Kedar Malla's house where he lived. Despite being tired on return from school he never neglected his studies. This apart, he used to offer his helping hand in the household works also. He was a sharp student and always stood first in his class. Besides studies he also took keen interest in other extra-curricular activities like, games and social works. His uncle Kedar Malla loved him very much as he was a sober and conscientious boy.

As he grew up to be an adult young man his talents in various field of music, literature and games unfolded themselves. He had a special flair for literary activities of reading and writing poems and articles. Through the poems he expressed deep sorrows and anguish for the condition of backwardness and ignorance of the society and tried to inspire people to rise and move forward towards progress. The tender heart of Durga Malla was greatly influenced by one Subedar Major Bahadur Singh Baral who was a poet and a social reformer besides being a retired soldier. The style and diction of his poems lavishly reflected in the writings of Durga Malla. He had special fascination for music and play-writes of master Mitra Sen whose Gramophone folk songs roused traditional ethos among the Indian Gorkhas. The most popular song of Master Mitra Sen – "Lahureko Relimaai" was much loved by Durga Malla and others.

He was proud of being a son of "Veer Gorkha" and earnestly

felt the need to uphold the tradition of bravery by the Gorkhas even at the cost of their lives. He hated cowardice and wanted that the Gorkhas should not be coward like other races. In the following poem written by him he gave vent to his profound disdain and desperation for the inertness and negative attitude assumed by the Gorkhas and implored them to rise from their slothful slumber and to follow the path of progress shown by others:

Dikhaao aakar Bhagwan, susupt jaati ko raah,
Kyaa huaa hamein, Kyon hui aaj mati mand;
Virata, pourush ke kaaran mili veer Gorkha ki upaadhi;
O hire ke samaan thaa ujjwal, kyon hua maati tulya,
Aaj dekhkar yeh, kuchh kah nahin saktaa;
Kab janeinge yah apne kartabya, sabhi ke udhe hai hosh.
Kaise milaa janam inhen, badal gaye saare;
Karate hain apnon ki chugli, pyaar baantne ke badle.
Chali gai purkhon ki pratisthaa, jaat hui badnaam;
Sirf bachaa hai maanab cholaa, kyon banaate ho maati.
'Durga' likh rahaa hai lekh, Prabhu choor karo inkaa darp;
Netra hon, to ab bhi dekho, annya logon ki chalne ki raah.

Durga Malla's adolescence period was marked by the advent of nationalist movement in India. In 1930s when Mahatma Gandhi had launched Civil Disobedience movement throughout India, Durga Malla was a smart and active young man eager to work for the welfare of the country and its people. He felt deeply disgraced by the subjugation of India by the British and wanted to join freedom movement of Mahatma Gandhi to free the country from the shackles of the foreign ruler. He heard about Gorkha youths who under the leadership of Khadak Bahadur Bist, a law student of Calcutta University, established secret nexus with the Gorkha soldiers in order to carry out revolutionary activities. He was also aware of Gandhiji's campaign of breaking the salt law when Khadag Bahadur Bist was arrested in May 1930 for attempting to loot the Government Salt Depot at Dharsana, 150 miles from Bombay and was imprisoned at Sabarmati jail together with his thirteen Gorkha associates. All these happenings boiled his young blood and roused extreme hatred towards the British. Dehradun, the hive of politically conscious Gorkha ex-servicemen was quick to join the nationalist movement launched by Congress leaders. From the early beginning of the twentieth century the Gorkhas of Dehradun evinced keen interest in the Arya Samaj movement led by Swami Dayananda Saraswati whose doctrine of 'Swaraja-Swabhasa-Swadharma' attracted the Gorkhas. (K.K. Muktan, *Legendary Gorkhas*, 2002) Through this organization they came under the influence of great leader like Lala Lajpat Rai who sowed the seed of socio-religious and nationalist ideas among the Gorkhas. Young Durga Malla was brought up and groomed under this socio-political scenario that prevailed in Dehradun during 1930s.

Service in the Army

While still a student, Durga Malla had to look for a job so that he could help his father to earn a livelihood for the family. In 1931 army recruitment started, as usual, at Dehradun and many young line boys including Durga Malla's friends got themselves recruited into Indian army. Durga Malla was just 18 years of age, the ripe age for army service. With his father's advice he joined the 2/1 Battalion of the Gorkha Rifles. Within stipulated time he successfully completed his training. A well trained, promising and a little more educated Durga Malla was selected for Signal Training. By dint of his dedication and sincerity he acquitted himself well in his service record and earned promotion to the responsible post of Signal Hawaldar within four years of service.

In 1941, at the age of 28 years, Durga Malla married Sharada Devi, a girl belonging to a Thakuri family of Kangrah, Himachal Pradesh. This was a time when the World War II had already begun. The thunder and fury of the war was raging in Britain, Greece, Yugoslavia, Albania, Russia etc. The Japanese army had already penetrated into Burma *via* Malaya. The Government of India had started sending out Indian army by consignments since October 1939 to fight at various war fronts all over the world. As for the Gorkha Rifles the Second World War was to become yet another landmark in its history of military service. Almost all the units of the ten Gorkha regiments took part in the war in different countries such as France, Germany, Italy, Burma. Hardly three days had passed after the marriage of Durga Malla when he was called back by his Unit to join his duty somewhere in Malaya war front. Duty bound as he was, as a disciplined soldier, Durga Malla, without being the least ruffled, left behind his newly married bride at home and proceeded to join his duty. His 2/1 Gorkha Rifles was ordered to depart for Malaya immediately. On 23 August, 1941 the battalion reached Bombay from Secundarabad and the next day it departed for Malaya from Bombay sea-port.

On 7 December, 1941 the Japanese aircraft struck the U.S naval base at Pearl Harbor on the island of Hawaii causing great destruction and damage to American battle-ships, aircrafts and other smaller vessels and killing 2403 people. (*Gurkha*, Peter Harclerode and David Reynolds, 2003 Gloucestershire, England, p.42) The following day, on 8 December, 1941 Japanese troops landed in Malaya and advanced towards the river Slim. Simultaneously, they carried out bombing raids on Singapore In Malaya Durga Malla's 2/1 Gorkha Rifles battalion together with 2/9 GR and other Indian regiments faced the first brunt of Japanese offensive across the Slim river. Fierce fighting ensued with gun shelling from both sides but superiority of number was on the enemy side. Within a matter of few hours the massive force of fifty Japanese tanks penetrated into Indian position. The Gorkhas fought bravely resisting the Japanese from advancing further but eventually failed to hold on. The enemy forces ruthlessly overran their position. Never before in the history of Indian army had the Indian soldiers felt so demoralized as did in Malaya and subsequently at other places in South-East Asia. The Indian forces had to retreat towards south to the fortress of Singapore to join the British and Australian columns. The Japanese launched a series of attacks, first on the Australian column on 8/9 February and then on the 11th Indian Division by a force of five thousand strong who infiltrated into the island under the cover of darkness. Unable to resist the onslaught the Australians withdrew from the front, thereby exposing the 11th Indian Division and leaving no choice for them but to follow the suit. Durga Malla and his men of the 2/1 GR and 2/2 GR were prepared to fight to the last man but to their utter disbelief and dismay, they received the order to lay down their weapons and surrender to the Japanese at 4 p.m. on 15th February, 1942. To surrender and to lay down arms to enemy is something emotionally unacceptable to the Gorkhas. They prefer to fight and die rather than surrender and that is the tradition set up by their predecessors. The motto of the Indian Gorkha Rifles is – 'Kaafar hunu bhandaa marnu niko' i.e., it is better to die than to be a coward. Thus, on their ignominious surrender, Singapore fell to the Japanese without resistance. A total of 85,000 British, Gorkhas, Indian and Australian troops were marched away into captivity on that infamous day. (*Gurkha*, Peter and David Reynolds, p. 44) Among the captured Indian troops were the remnants of the 2/2 GR and 2/1 Gorkha Rifles including Durga Malla, the Signal Hawaldar and many of his fellow Gorkha soldiers. That was the first ever shock which struck the heart of Durga Malla who took pride of being a Veer Gorkha.

On the Burma sector the Japanese forces crossed the Burma-Siam border on 16 December, 1941 and captured Victoria Point. By 5 March, 1942 the Japanese forces succeeded in crossing the Sittang river and at this point they branched out into two Divisions – one heading south-west *via* Pegu to Rangoon, while the other advanced towards the west to join the former at Rangoon. Before reaching Rangoon, at Magaung they met with a Gorkha column which put up a stiff resistance, determined not to allow an inch to advance forward. The Gorkhas fought doggedly and laid down their lives. Havildar Tul Bahadur Pun, the lone survivor of his platoon went on firing from his bren-gun without regard to his personal safety, wading through deep mud and killing three Japanese and capturing five more with two machine-guns. Later on Tul Bahadur Pun was awarded Victoria Cross, the highest gallantry award in military service. On March 7, 1942 both the Divisions of Japanese forces reached Rangoon and captured the capital of Burma, without resistance as the British and the Indian army had already withdrawn by themselves. The captured and surrendered Indian troops were transported to Singpore to form part of the INA as per plan mooted out by Captain Mohan Singh and Major Fujiwara.

In the I.N.A.

After the fall of Singapore to the Japanese of 15 February, 1942 the next day, on 17 February 85,000 POWs, consisting of surrendered and captured British Indian army were marched to Farrer Park where Major Fukiwara, the Chief of Intelligence of the Japanese army addressed them inviting them to join the INA for the liberation of their country India. Captain Mohan Singh, the Indian army officer captured earlier by Japanese, delivered a spirited speech explaining the objectives of INA and requesting the POWs to take the opportunity to drive away the British from India by military force with the help of Japanese army. He called upon the Indian soldiers to join the INA and after conclusion of the speech he shouted the slogan — "Jai Hind, Jai Bharat." Reciprocating him, majority of the POWs spontaneously cried out – Jai Hind, Jai Bharat and — raised their hands indicating their willingness to join the INA. Durga Malla, among the Gorkhas, was the first to raise his hand. He did so because the seed of nationalism was already sown in him when he was still a student in Dehradun and he well understood the meaning and purpose of the mission. Some other Gorkhas such as Dal Bahadur Thapa, Mohan Thapa, Man Singh, Mohan Singh Gorkha, etc., also followed him to join the INA as they were India born line boys. But many of the Gorkha POWs were not in favour of joining the INA as they found it hard to change side on the ground of Gorkha loyalty and fidelity. Durga Malla and his followers took the initiative to motivate and induce them to fall in line with the main course and finally all the Gorkha POWs joined the INA.

In the INA Durga Malla and his fellow Gorkha soldiers played a crucial role. Most of the Gorkhas were enlisted in the Bahadur Group of the INA which, as a striking force of the INA was responsible to take the lead in the offensives. It was the Bahadur Group which took the leading role in attacking and breaking the British Indian column while advancing towards Imphal and Kohima. It was this Bahadur Group again which suffered the heaviest casualties. Naik Man Bahadur Thapa of the 1st Bahadur Group was killed in action during the offensive in the Arakan. Havildar Sital Bahadur of the 1st Bahadur Group was killed in a hand to hand fight against the British force near Ramakori, Burma in August 1944. Rifleman Kalu Gorkha of the 1st Bahadur Group died by drowning while swimming across the river Sittang after its bridge was blown up by the order of Major General Smyth of the Indian army in order to prevent further advancement of the Japanese force. Captain Sher Bahadur Bhandari who belonged to Durga Malla's 2/1 Gorkha Rifles and joined INA together with him, was seriously injured during the fight near Rangoon and died later in Burma Hospital. He was also in the Bahadur Group. Thus we find in record as many as twenty-five Gorkha soldiers who laid down their lives fighting against the British force. These were only a few Gorkha soldiers whose names were recorded by Dr. P.N. Chopra, in his book – *Who is Who of Indian Martyrs*, Vol. I, 1969 but there were many more others of the INA Gorkhas who were killed in encounter, maimed and missing whose names are either not known or not recorded. There were also a good number of Gorkha soldiers who acquitted themselves well in the war and received *Azad Hind Fauz* awards and medals for their fighting spirits and show of extraordinary bravery and absolute contempt for danger. A list of these brave Gorkhas has been furnished separately at the Appendix-II.

Lieutenant Durga Malla was an enthusiastic and enterprising propagandist who was awarded 'Sanad E-Bahadur' medal by Netaji himself for his bravery and outstanding performance of espionage duty. The following extract taken from the book of K.S. Giani – *Indian Independence Movement in East Asia*, 1947, Lahore, speaks loudly about Durga Malla's high sense of responsibility and sheer contempt for death in the accomplishment of duty:

> " As the war was blazing in the Arakan hills an order was issued from INA Headquarters that one should immediately be deputed for anti-British propaganda work in the enemy camp on the other side of the hillock. Lieutenant Durga Bahadur volunteered himself for this mission. He disguised as a Gorkha officer of the Indian army and crossed over to the enemy post risking his life. There he made personal contacts with the Gorkha soldiers, held secret talks, passed on the bundles of INA pamphlets and returned back successfully to his camp the next morning. Lieutenant Durga Bahadur was awarded 'Sanad E-Bahadur' by Netaji for his gallant enterprise in March 1944".

Durga Malla was also promoted to the rank of Major for his meritorious service and made in-charge of Intelligence Branch of the INA. He, together with a group of Gorkha intelligence squad entered into the hilly areas of Burma-Assam border for espionage work. There he was engaged in collecting secret and strategically important information with the help of his team and maintained a close liaison with INA Headquarters at Rangoon as well as with the B.V. (Secret wing of the Forward Block) in Calcutta Office. This fact is proved by the following abstract taken from Leonard A. Gordon's, *Brothers Against Raj*, New Delhi, 1990, pp. 476-77.

> " It may be noted how the B.V. arose out of the 1928 Calcutta Congress and how they remained devoted to Bose through the 1930s. .... Then B.V. men tried to send operatives across the frontiers to Burma in 1943 and 1944 and Bose, with Japanese assistance tried to send small groups of men equipped with wireless into India. Most of these groups were caught, some imprisoned and a few executed".

On one fateful day on 27 March, 1944 when Durga Malla was on an important mission of collecting information from within the camp area of the 10th Division of Indian army at Ukhrul, he was caught red handed with a wireless set and some propaganda materials in his possession. He was identified to be one of the surrendered soldier of the 2/1 Gorkha Rifles who joined the INA and was brought to Delhi for imprisonment and trial.

Prosecution and Trial

Durga Malla was prosecuted by the Military court under section 41 of the Indian Army Act and section 121 of the Indian Penal Code for waging war against the King-Emperor. The trial was held by the Court Martial of Indian army at the historic Red Fort of New Delhi. On the first day Durga Malla was brought before the Court Martial under the army escort and made to stand on the improvised dock. He looked stern, unruffled and grave and faced direct towards the army top brasses forming the Court Martial. The Presiding Officer of the Court explained the charges levelled by the prosecution to Durga Malla and asked him to answer as to whether he was guilty of the charges or not. Durga Malla's reply came forth instantly in clear and confident voice that he was guilty of the charges. Amazed and somewhat indignated Presiding officer, discharging his legal imperatives, warned Durga Malla that if he confessed the offences committed by him under section 121 of the Indian Penal Code he would be liable for the punishment of death and, therefore, he should, think about it before he gives his reply. Durga Malla, however, seemed adamant in his stand and would not fear death punishment. After a short discussion the Court Martial decided to give some time to Durga Malla to think over and to appear before the court on the next date. Unfortunately, there was no legal adviser, nor any lawyer to counsel him or to defend the case of Durga Malla, in which event the proceedings of the court might have taken a different turn. But Durga Malla, left to himself, continued to maintain the same stand and boldly confessed his guilt when brought before the court on the next date of hearing. It may be mentioned that during the trial of three other top ranking INA officers, viz., Colonel Prem Sahgal, Colonel Gurubaksh Singh Dhillon and Major General Shah Nawaz Khan who were charged with the same offence under Sections of the Indian Penal Code a number of eminent lawyers of India including Jawaharlal Nehru, Bhulabhai Desai, Kailashnath Katju, etc., came forward to defend them and on being convicted by the Court-Martial, the matter was made a political issue and great public agitation was raged. This situation ultimately led the British Government to withdraw the conviction of them all. But for a petty Gorkha soldier like Durga Malla no one bothered to come forward for help. So, on 15 August, 1944, the Court Martial finally pronounced its judgement convicting Durga Malla under section 121 of the Indian Penal Code and sentencing him to be hanged until death. Gallant Durga Malla received the sentence with absolute calm and cool demeanour. A brave soldier, indeed, was he. He preferred to embrace death rather than telling what was not true and get away, for he thought that he joined the INA for liberation of India and to die for the country was a matter of great virtue. His young wife was brought to see him for the last time in the prison cell who fell at his feet weeping and wailing. Durga Malla helped her on to her feet and consoled her telling – " Sharada, I am sacrificing my life for the freedom of my country ; so do not weep, but take it from me that my sacrifice will not go in vain ; India will be free from British rule and millions of Hindustanis will be with you.

Early dawn, on 25 August, 1944 Durga Malla, the freedom fighter and great son of India, was led to the gallows and hanged until death. Thus ended the life of a Gorkha soldier who made a supreme sacrifice for the country and became immortal. Today India remembers Durga Malla as a martyr and pays homage to him by observing Martyr Day (Balidan Divas) on 25 August every year. An eighteen feet high bronze statue of this great hero stands erected within the Indian Parliament House premises depicting Veer Durga Malla riding on a galloping horse with a bare Khukhri in his hand. This statue was constructed under the aegis of the Bharatiya Gorkha Parisangha, the only all India representative body of the Indian Gorkhas and was unveiled by Dr. Man Mohan Singh, Prime Minister of India on 17 December, 2004 in the presence of Bhairon Singh Shekhawat, Vice-President of India, Ms. Sonia Gandhi, President of Indian National Congress, Somnath Chatterjee, Speaker of Lok Sabha and many dignitories.

End Result of the INA War

The end result of the INA struggle for freedom eventually proved to be a positive one. What Shaheed Durga Malla had predicted came to be true. India became free on the 15th August, 1947, within three years of the execution of Durga Malla as the British willingly handed over power to Indian leaders without further political agitation. The supreme sacrifice made by him and so many other INA soldiers did not go in vain.

The INA war against the British army, might have well, ended in failure but it left a tremendous impact on the psyche of the colonial ruler. The suicide squad led by Col. Saukat Malik on 18 April, 1944 broke through the British defence and captured Moirang in Manipur. The INA took control of Moirang and hoisted the first flag on INA on the Indian soil. The INA also breached the Kohima road posing a potential threat to British position in both Silchar and Kohima. Col. Gulzara Singh's column had penetrated 250 miles into Indian territory. This was enough show of strength to the British army which Indian troops are capable of. This apart, the act of changing sides by the Indian troops captured by Japanese and the subsequent rebellion of Royal Indian Navy in 1946 did cast a terrible doubt about their trustworthiness. Mr. Attlee, the

Prime Minister of Great Britain himself had very well realized the vulnerability of the British dominion over India when he ruefully said :

> "Among the principal reasons the one was the erosion of loyalty to British Crown among the Indian army and Navy personnel as a result of military activities of Netaji."

Thus the arms struggle by Netaji, although was costly, struck the final blow to the British Government and shook the very foundation of imperialism.

7

Gorkhas in Kargil War

The Background History

The independence of India in 1947 entailed division of the country into two dominions, viz., India and Pakistan. The Indian sub-continent, as it was called then, was partitioned into two halves along the religious lines followed by large scale movement of people from one country to another as repatriation of population. There were another 650 odd princely States which were also destined to group themselves in either sides. As a principle these Princely States had the option of deciding which country to join or of remaining independent States. However in practice, the restive population of these States did not allow the princes to go by their own choice in selecting the country. Although many princes wanted to remain independent they had to succumb to the desire of the people in joining a new country.

The princely State of Jammu and Kashmir was ruled by Maharaja Hari Singh, a Hindu King of Dogra dynasty while the majority of its population were Muslims. Unable to decide which country to join Hari Singh choose to remain neutral. Taking the opportunity, Mahammad Ali Jinnah, Governor-General of Pakistan planned to annex Jammu and Kashmir into Pakistan by force overthrowing the Dogra ruler. He stirred religious sentiments of *Jehad* (holy war) among the Muslim population and inducted thousands of Pathan tribesmen from the North-West Frontier against the Hindu ruler of Kashmir. The turbulent Pathans stormed into the gorge of Jhelum river, seized Muzaffarabad and Domel and went on to sack Baramula, situated less than sixty kilometres from Srinagar. Hari Singh, the Maharaja finding no other alternative signed the instrument of accession ceding Jammu &

Kashmir into Indian Union on October 26, 1947. Pandit Jawaharlal Nehru, Prime Minister of India declared in the Parliament—"since the State of Jammu and Kashmir has formally ceded to India it was our responsibility to see that the State was protected at all costs as a part of our country."

On October 27, 1947 Indian troops were flown to Srinagar and then to Baramula. The Pakistani army which was so long acting behind the scene by providing necessary arms and ammunitions and training the Pathans came out openly to fight the Indian soldiers. The following month Indian army succeeded in pushing back the Pakistani troops and retaking Baramula.The conflict now developed into full scale war.

In January 1948 the 2/3rd Gorkha Rifles moved to Samba, an important junction on the Pathankot Jammu-Srinagar road. The Battalion was then posted along a ten-mile stretch of the Indo-Pakistan border to check enemy infiltration. By the onset of monsoon the Uri-Mahura sector became very active with frequent enemy firing. So the 2/3rd Gorkha Rifles immediately took over all the piquets and posts from the Rajputana Rifles. On June 28, 1948 the 2/3rd Gorkha Rifles captured Pirkanthi, a 10,930 feet high strategic feature strongly held by Pakistani troops. The Gorkha boys, under the leadership of gallant Company Commander, Major K.S. Rana charged the enemy in a determined swoop with khukris, bayonets and grenades wreaking dreadful carnage until the enemy broke and fled the scene. In this battle Major K.S. Rana, Lance Naik Purna Bahadur and Rifleman Jas Bahadur Thapa won Vir Chakra for their gallantry.

The Pakistani army started large concentration of troops in preparation to capture Leh and Skordu. In May and June two companies of Gorkhas were flown to Leh where a massive attack by a thousand Pakistani force was successfully repulsed by the Gorkhas and Leh was protected.

As the armed conflict went on unabated the Government of India referred the dispute to the United Nations for intervention on the 1st January, 1948. The UN in its resolution dated 13 August, 1948 asked Pakistan to withdraw its troops after which India also removed bulk of its forces. But Pakistan ignored UN mandate and continued to fight till January 1, 1949 when a seize-fire was agreed upon between the two sides. On this date about 65 per cent of the territory was under India while the rest were in Pakistani control. It was at this stage the line of control (LOC) was set up and since then this LOC has become a de fucto border between India and Pakistan. In 1957 the State of Jammu & Kashmir was formally incorporated into the Indian Union and granted special status under Article 370 of the Constitution which ensures, among other things, that non-Kashmiri Indian cannot buy property in Kashmir.

In 1972 Smt. Indira Gandhi, Prime Minister of India and Mr. Julfikar Ali Bhutto, Prime Minister of Pakistan signed an important agreement in Simla through which both the countries agreed to stop all kinds of infiltration into each other's sides or armed conflict and to hold peaceful dialogues in order to resolve amicably all outstanding disputes regarding Kashmir. This historic agreement is known as Simla Agreement and it remains in force till today.

Looking into the matter under the light of the historical background as narrated above it will appear that Pakistani army's infiltration into the Indian soil across the border defined by the LOC and illegal occupation of Kargil by constructing permanent bunkers is nothing sort of an act of invasion of Indian territory From this point of view the war waged by the Indian army in 1999 to liberate Kargil from the foreign occupation can be termed as yet another freedom struggle.

Kargil War, 1999 (A Freedom Struggle)

Kargil, a sparsely populated town in the district of Ladakh and is situated on the Indian side of the Line of Control (LOC) as mandated on 13th August, 1948 resolution of the United Nations and accepted as such by both India and Pakistan. It is 205 kilometres away from Srinagar and stands on the Indian National Highway (NH10) connecting Srinagar with Leh. For this reason Kargil assumes a politically very strategic position and militarily a significant logistical situation.

During the winter months of 1999 when patrolling by Indian troops was less frequent due to extreme cold in the high mountain region, the Pakistani troops, in a calculated move to grab the strategic Kargil hills crossed the LOC and established a number of permanent bunkers. The Indian intelligence and the border security organization were blissfully ignorant about this for a number of months. On the 14th May, 1999 the nation was shocked to learn about it when the Pakistani intruders captured an Indian patrolling party of five Indian soldiers including one Lieutenant Saurabh Kalia and killed them in a most barbaric way after they were meted out inhuman treatment in captivity is blatant violation of Geneva Convention. Later on their mutilated bodies were returned back to Indian army. It also came to light that the intruders were not Kashmiri militants as claimed by Islamabad but they were foreign mercenaries from Afghanistan mixed with Pakistani army regulars. They had built three storied pucca bunkers equipped with power generator around Kargil several kilometres inside the line of control. Trenches had been dug and many posts built up connecting them with roads on their side of the Loc. They had stored ammunitions including shoulder-fired surface to air stinger missiles and stored provisions that would last for several months. Such a meticulous arrangement made by the invaders proved beyond doubt that the intrusion had taken place months before without a shred of knowledge of the Indian side. On the 27th May 1999, an Indian MIG 21 was shot down well within Indian side of the LOC by Pakistani shoulder to air stinger and Flight Lieutenant K. Nachiketa was captured.

All these developments made the situation extremely emergent and provocative to Indian army. However, the enemy positions were very difficult to tackle by land force. The topography of the enemy position gave them extra logistic advantage. The Pakistani posts being located on top of high mountain ranging between 15,000 to 18,000 feet above which was logistically impossible to dislodge them. The Tiger hill located only four kilometres away from the LOC was one of the most strategic posts held by the enemy which had a dominating command over the Srinagar-Leh Highway, the life-line of Indian defence. The Tiger Hill rose steeply ending in a conical shape with no spur or ridgelines on either sides which rendered climbing most difficult. Even a small force of 25 to 30 men sitting atop the peak could hold more than a Brigade— said Col. A.S. Chebrewal of the 8th Mountain Division. Pakistani plan was to occupy the advantageous points on the top of the high ridges overlooking Srinagar-Leh road, to snap communication system and to capture Siachin region. Their plan was, however, frustrated by powerful Indian air strikes which proved to be effective encounter which Pakistani army had never thought of. The Indian Air Force combat jets and helicopter gun-ships launched their sorties and air strikes over the enemy posts in Kargil and Drass sectors pounding and destroying the enemy hide-outs not sparing their stores and provisions. While doing so extreme care and restraint was taken to see that not a single bomb was dropped on the other side of the LOC. Side by side with air strikes Indian land force started artillery shelling from below and advancing towards the enemy posts. Heavy fighting continued in all sectors. Indian jawans fought heroically inflicting heavy casualties on the invaders. On June 8, 1999, after a fierce gun battle in Kargil sector Indian troops achieved a major success by recapturing two main features in Batalik subsector. The troops gunned down thirteen Pakistani infiltrators and pushed the remainders back to the close of the LOC. India lost three jawans in this encounter. The intruders were dislodged from the Tiger hills and Tololing sectors also but they shifted to new positions in Kaksur and Batalik sectors making it difficult to flush out completely without crossing the LOC. General V. N. Sarma (Retired) said that unless the intruders were encircled from the other side of the LOC it would mean a continuous operation involving heavy casualties. Another military expert opined that India was fighting a war in which the time, place and scope of operation were being decided by Pakistan. The issue of crossing the LOC hanged on indecision until 24th June, 1999, when Atal Bihari Bajpayee, Prime Minister of India finally set the speculation at rest by announcing that the sanctity of the Line of Control would be respected. In spite of the nefarious intention of Pakistan, the Indian policy of restraint by maintaining the sanctity of the LOC and her ever readiness to promote good neighbourly relationship with Pakistan paid a rich dividend. The international community took the side of India as one body and censured Pakistan for its ill-conceived political agenda. Pakistan was isolated from the international comity of nations. British expressed deep concern over the infiltration of foreign mercenaries in Kargil and urged India and Pakistan to de-escalate the situation. A ten member ASEAN (Association of the South East Asian countries) backed India's stand on the Kargil issue and asked both India and Pakistan to resolve the dispute through dialogue. The US Secretary of State Madeliene Albright told a crowded press conference in Singapore that Pakistan should withdraw from Kargil and stop further terrorism. Even China, Pakistan's ally failed to appreciate Nawaz

Sharif's action and asked him to resolve the dispute through peaceful means.

On 17 June, 1999 Indian Air Force further intensified its attack on the intruders position in Kargil and recaptured Tololing peak that was strongly held by the enemy. In the operation Major Ajay Singh Jasrotia and a jawan laid down their lives after fighting bravely and killing eight Pakistani troops and wounding nine others. A major success was achieved on 20th June, 1999 when Indian jawans recaptured peak No. 5140 under the able leadership of Captain Bikram Batra of 13th Jammu & Kashmir Rifles. Gallant Bikram Batra, however, lost his life in subsequent encounter for which he was awarded posthumously the country's highest gallantry award of Param Vir Chakra.

The 11th Gorkha Rifles played an important role in Kargil war operation, as they did on earlier occasion. This was the second time that the Gorkhas fought against the Pakistani forces in these inhospitable snow capped mountains of Kargil. It reminded them how in 1948 the Gorkha boys stormed upon the Pathan tribesmen and Pakistani regulars along Kargil borders with khukries and bayonets wreaking a carnage and pushing the enemy back until they become demoralized and flee the battle ground. It was on 26th June, 1948 that the 2/3rd Gorkha Rifles under the command of Major K.S. Rana launched a decisive attack on the Pakistani post at Pirkanthi. This time around although their target was very steep and difficult to climb and they were almost swept away by the enemy shelling, the Gorkhas disregard of their life risk rushed forward inflicting heavy casualties to the enemy. They lost two men of their side, viz, Lance Naik Purna Bahadur Thapa and Rifleman Jas Bahadur Thapa, but succeeded in capturing the enemy post.

Recounting his experience Rifleman A. Gurung says — on the 10th June, 1999 we headed for the Peak No. 5040 which was the immediate target of our assault. As we started climbing the peak we came under heavy enemy shelling from the top. Our position was so vulnerable that our opponents from the top could count our heads. Undaunted, we pushed forward and gave roaring reply with our M.M.Gs. guarding ourselves against rocks and bushes whatever we find at hand. I shot four Pakistani dead and before I could refill my MMG for the next round I was hit by a mortar in my leg and was bleeding profusely while I saw Major Tripathy by my side hit by a bullet on his head. The next moment there was darkness in my eyes, my head whirled and I fell unconscious until I woke up to find myself in the army hospital.

When fierce fighting was ravaging in the Kargil sector two Gorkha soldiers of 4/5 Gorkha regiment Ram Bahadur Gurung and Jim Bahadur Thapa lost their lives together with seven others in a train bomb blast at New Jalpaiguri on 22nd June, 1999. The train was carrying Indian troops to Kargil and it was an act of sabotage by Pakistani ISI (Inter Service intelligence) against the movement of Indian soldiers to Kargil. Rifleman Vijoy Gurung who was seriously injured in the blast was fighting a grim battle for life in Calcutta hospital when he said— "I do not regret, for I am a Gorkha soldier destined to die. I still wish to join the Kargil war and kill Pakistani intruders after getting well.

During 'Operation Vijoy' in Kargil the Gorkha soldiers of the 11th Gorkha regiment and the 2nd Nagaland Regiment played crucial part in the fight and showed extreme courage, skill and determination. They also suffered the maximum casualties. The Gorkhas sacrificed as many as twenty-two precious lives of which (to specify regiment-wise) eight killed from 11th Gorkha Regiment, six from Nagaland Regiment, five from 4th and three from the 3rd Gorkha Rifles. It may be made clear at this juncture that all the twnty-two Gorkhas who laid down their lives in the operation were the sons of Indian Nepalis settled in India and none from Nepal. Most of the parents were third or fourth generation Indian Nepalis who retired from Indian army. Undoubtedly, it is a unique contribution for a single community to sacrifice so many lives for the sake of the country in one operation. The following paragraphs highlight, in brief, on the saga of valour and sacrifice of the young Gorkha jawans who gave their lives for the country.

Havildar Man Bahadur Rai of 6/11 Gorkha Rifles together with his Gorkha jawans launched a gallant and determined offensive on the Pakistani intruders on the 12th June, 1999, and inflicted heavy casualties to the enemy. During the course of fighting Man Bahadur Rai rushed forward leading his men against heavy enemy shelling and in complete disregard of his personal safety when he received a fatal injury and succumbed to it.His mortal remain was brought to Sukia Pokhari, Darjeeling, his home town and cremated on 18th June, 1999 with full military honour. His widowed wife Lolita Rai proudly said — "I am a daughter of Vir Gorkha, I'll not cry. I'll rather send my only son to the war to avenge his father's death.

Earlier on the 15th May, 1999 another Gorkha jawan Suniljong Mahat of 1/11 Gorkha Rifles be-came a martyr after fighting bravely in Kargil sector. He comes of a traditional army family. His grand father Major Nakul Mahat served in the Jammu-Kashmir Regiment from 1921 to 1961 and after retirement settled at Kangra in Himachal Pradesh. He had eleven sons all of whom served in the Indian army. Suniljong's father was the tenth son who is now working in Lucknow after retirement from army.

In the same encounter in Kargil sector another brave son of a brave father laid down his life for the country. His name was Mekh Bahadur Gurung of 1/11 Gorkha Rifles. His father Ram Bahadur Gurung was in the Indian army and fought at various theatres of war during Chinese aggression in 1962 and Bangladesh war of 1971 and earned many a laurel. This brave hearted exserviceman was proud of his son who died in the battle ground fighting bravely. Rifleman Mekh Bahadur was born and brought up in the military ambience at Dehra Dun army cantonment and received education from the 58 GTC Junior High School.

Two young boys Rifleman Linkon Pradhan of Sukia Pokhari, Darjeeling and Arun Kumar Rai of Sonada. Darjeeling joined army in the 1/11 Gorkha Rifles together in 1999 and received training together. They were hardly twenty years of age when they fought their first and the last battle of life at Kargil with courage and determination. Rifleman Linkon Pradhan was making a desperate attempt to climbe the hill top braving against shower of enemy bullets but was hit by a gun shot on his head and fell dead. His friend Rifleman Arun Kumar Rai was killed on the 3rd July, 1999 in a similar attempt to repulse the enemy from their position. In the tragic death of these two young soldiers their wives Smt. Kavita Pradhan and Smt. Vijoya Rai were left as widows at a very prime of their lives.

In another encounter with Pakistani intruders Rifleman Ramesh Thapa of 2/3 Gorkha Rifles fought heroically and gave his life in the Drass sector on the 3rd July, 1999. His dead body was brought to his village Haripur Kanwali, Dehra Dun and cremated with full military honour. The public of Haripur named one of their village roads as Shaheed Ramesh Thapa road in the honour of this brave martyr.

The most crucial battle of this series was, however, fought in the Moskoh valley and Tiger hill in the first week of July, 1999 in which Indian jawans gave a decisive blow to the Pakistani troops and pushed them back to the Line of Control. The casualties on both sides were colossal. The Gorkhas alone lost as many as seven jawans at various places of fighting. In one of these encounters two companies of 1/11 Gorkha Rifles advanced towards the Peak No. 4812 on second July under the command of Col. Lalit Rai. As they reached about 800 metres short of the peak the Pakistani forces greeted them with shower of heavy shelling. Undaunted by this the Gorkhas pressed forward in their counter attack. The Commanding Officer took the lead with six bodyguards one of whom was Havilder Gyan Bahadur Tamang. As they got at a point barely 200 metres away from their target the Pakistani forces intensified firing of which a splinter pierced the neck of Havildar Gyan Bahadur Tamang. Not caring for the injury and his personal safety he maintained close guard with his Commander and in the process killing Pakstani soldiers with his LMG. Soon he found himself soaked in blood and too weak to fight. So he jumped down five metres below to find a safer place. Hurriedly he tore out his vest and tied up the injured neck so as to stop heavy flow of blood and then he jumped out of his hiding and sprayed bullets to the enemy killing three Pakistani invaders.

On the night of 6th July, 1999 a fierce fighting took place at Moskoh valley between Second Nagaland Regiment and Pakistani troops. The redoubtable Gorkhas and Naga jawans of this regiment under the able leadership of their Commander launched a massive attack on the enemy undaunted by the logistic disadvantage they had to face. Heavy shelling from both sides continued throughout the night when the Indian troops inflicted heavy casualties to Pakistanis compelling them to retreat back to near LOC. In this encounter Indian side lost eight jawans which include three Gorkhas. Rifleman Sanjoy Gurung showed extreme courage and skill when he continued to fire through his LMG killing Pakistani soldiers despite bullet injuries received by him and until he became exhausted and fell dead. When the sad news of Sanjoy Gurung's death was broken to his father Hav. Meher Singh Gurung he reacted calmly saying—This was expected to happen one day. While in military service I have seen many deaths from close quarters. One son of mine has given his life for the country, I am ready to sacrifice all the three sons who are now in the army.

Rifleman Ratan Kumar Pradhan was another Gorkha who fell to enemy bullets during the Kargil operation. He belonged to Second Nagaland Regiment and fought valiantly in close company with Sanjoy Gurung. The third Gorkha jawan who met with the same fate was Rajesh Gurung. He also belonged to the same Second Nagaland Regiment which played an important role in the Kargil war of 1999. His mortal remain was brought to his village Chandmari, Dehra Dun where his father, ex-serviceman Shyan Singh Gurung received the coffin with sprightly military salute. Shyam Singh Gurung himself was a hero of many such battles in Bangladesh in 1971 and Jammu & Kashmir in 1965 and had not forgotten the horrors of war. He said — At this moment my blood boils up and longs to join Kargil war to avenge the death of my son. The public of Dehra Dun dedicated a road in the name of Rajesh Gurung whose mother Basanti Devi Gurung lights a lamp by the side of this road every evening in her son's loving memory.

The Second Nagaland Regiment, the youngest regiment of the Indian army (raised in 1964) bore the brunt of the Operation Vijoy and suffered the highest casualty in terms of man and materials. Hav. Mohan Pun Magar, Naik Hari Bahadur Ghale and Rifleman Suresh Chhetri of this regiment immortalized their names and upheld the tradition of their regiment by fighting bravely and sacrificing their lives for the motherland. Naik Hari Bahadur Ghale fell to the enemy bullet while engaged in heavy gun battle in Moshkoh valley on the 6th July, 1999. Hav. Mohan Pun Magar was killed on the 7th July in the Moshkoh valley while Suresh Chhetri went down fighting in the Tiger hills sector on the 7th July together with seven other Indian jawans. Smt. Manju Chhetri, 22 years old wife of martyr Suresh Chhetri, when asked said, — I am pregnant and I wish I have a son so that I may send him to army to follow the foot-steps of his father." A brave wife of a brave Gorkha soldier. In a condolence massage to her the Union Minister for Defence, Mr. George Fernandez wrote — "Your husband Suresh Chhetri laid down his life for the country like a brave soldier".

Naik Krishna Bahadur Thapa of the 3/4th Gorkha Rifles was killed in the Operation Vijoy on the 11th July, 1999 while fighting in the Drass sector. His father Captain Mohan Singh Thapa was a retired army officer of Dehra Dun who said that he was proud of his son to lay down his life for the country.

Another young Gorkha soldier who laid down his life for Mother India was Rifleman Phurba Tamang of Kalimpong. He had joined 4/4 Gorkha Rifles only in 1992 and had fought the war for the first time. He left behind his young wife Sunita Tamang and a nine months old daughter when he went down fighting in the Batalik sector on the 23rd August, 1999.

The saga of valour and sacrifice will not be complete if we do not mention the names of the following brave Gorkha soldiers who took part in various sectors of Kargil war at different times and laid down their precious lives. They are — Rifleman Birendra Thapa of 5/3 GR. Rifleman Ashish Thapa (24 yearas), Rifleman Manish Thapa (22 years), Rifleman Deepraj Pradhan (26 years), Rifleman Dibakar Tamang (25 years), Rifleman Kritagna Singh Rana, and Rifleman Dal Bahadur Pun.

Thus, the Gorkhas played a crucial role in the Kargil war of 1999. By the end of June, 1999 the Indian army had retaken almost all the important positions and expelled the invaders from Indian territories. Behind this spectacular success was, undoubtedly, the saga of extreme courage and supreme sacrifice of the Gorkha and Indian jawans. The Pakistani intruders who had so strongly fortified themselves on the hill tops could not have been dislodged so easily within a short span to two months, had it not been for the valour and skill of these redoubtable soldiers. More than 400 jawans of the Indian army laid down their lives of which 22 were Gorkhas, which is a unique contribution to India for one community alone.

8

Freedom Fighter Captain Ram Singh Thakuri

Captain Ram Singh Thakuri was born on 15 August, 1914 in a small village named Khanyara in the district of Dharamsala, Uttar Pradesh (now Himachal Pradesh) in a Gorkha family. Dharamsala or Bhagru being the Headquarters of the Gorkha regiment so he was brought up in military ambience of the Gorkha society. It was a tradition among the Gorkhas of Dharamsala to send their sons to serve in the army after they grow up to their eligible age. Therefore, Ram Singh also joined the army in the First Gorkha Rifles immediately after he completed his school education in the local High School. Ram Singh possessed an uncanny interest and talent in music since his childhood and learnt to play on violin, harmonium and percussion band. So immediately after he joined the service he was taken into the military band Unit. Within a short time he could demonstrate extraordinary professionalism in music composition, devotion to duty and discipline. For this reason he was promoted to the rank of Havildar Major.

During World War II when the Japanese army made their incursion in Malaya in 1940 and advanced towards Burma after crossing the river Slim the British Government of India dispatched Indian army to check the advancement of the Japanese under the leadership of Major General Smyth. Among the Indian army there were many Gorkha regiments. In September 1941, Havildar Major Ram Singh's Ist Gorkha Rifles together with his Band Unit also joined the war in Burma. Ram Singh Thakuri rendered great service in the war by inspiring his regiment with his extraordinary military band for which he was awarded the 'King George VI medal'. The Gorkha soldiers launched a determined offensive to stall the advancing Japanese force on the western bank of river Slim. A fierce battle ensued with gun shelling from both sides but the superiority of number was on the enemy side. Within a matter of a few hours the massive force of Japanese tanks penetrated into Indian position and almost routed them back. The Gorkhas, nevertheless, fought bravely with heavy casualties but could not resist the Japanese who ruthlessly overran Indian position and captured many Indian troops including Gorkhas who were taken as prisoners of war.

On the 16th December, 1941 the Japanese finally crossed Burma-Siam border and captured the Victoria Point held by British army. They pushed back the Indian troops foiling their weak resistance under Major General Smyth and advanced towards Rangoon and captured the capital of Burma. In the process, the Japanese army took a large number Indian soldiers as POWs.

On 15 February, 1942 Singapore too fell to the enemy after the surrender of British army. The following day a large number of British and Indian soldiers laid down their arms. Altogether there were 85,000 British and Indian soldiers including Gorkhas who became the prisoners of war. This figure included those who surrendered on earlier occasions in Malaya. On the 17th February Major Fukiwara of the Japanese army and Captain Mohan Singh, a surrenderee of Indian army, addressed the POWs in a meeting held at Ferrar Park of Singapore. In the meeting the speakers explained the purpose of the Indian National Army and enlisted the POWs in the INA. After a few days of procrastination the captured Gorkhas were also inspired with the spirit of nationalism and joined the INA. Most of the Gorkhas who readily decided to support the cause of India's liberation were the sons of Indian Nepalis settled in various parts of India since generations. Captain Ram Singh Thakuri also joined the INA with his Band Unit.

Subhas Chandra Bose took over the leaderhip of the INA on 4th July, 1943 and reorganised the force into a large and powerful army with the enlistment Indian expatriates of the South Asia under the new nomenclature of 'Azad Hind Fouz'. In the INA Ram Singh Thakuri and his Unit played a crucial role. Netaji Subhas Chandra Bose praised his music talent and promoted him to the rank of Captain. At the request of Netaji Subhas Bose, Ram Singh Thakuri rendered martial tune to the poem of Rabindranath Tagore —*'Jana gana mana adhinayaka jaiya he'* — He orchestrated this song in full military band for the first time on October 21, 1943 before a largely attended function held at Darbar Hall of the famous Cathay Building of Singapore. Netaji Subhas Chandra Bose so loved the song that he adopted it as the National Song of the interim Azad Hind Government. Some sections of the people claim that this song was composed by Ram Singh Thakuri himself for the INA but this has been contradicted by others asserting that it was composed by poet Rabindranath Tagore. After India obtained independence in 1947 this song was adopted as the National Anthem of India to commemorate the glorious war of independence fought by INA soldiers and their supreme sacrifice for the country.

Credit also goes to Captain Ram Singh Thakuri for the composition of the famous marching song — *'Kadam kadam badhaye ja, khusi ke geet gaye ja'* — which inspired patriotic feeling among the INA soldiers during their grim battle against the Japanese in Burma. Today this song has become so popular in India that it is played by Indian military and almost all para-military forces on every national function. Captain Ram Sing composed and tuned this song by himself especially for INA. Captain Ram Singh also composed many other patriotic songs like *'Sukh such-chain'* or *'Quami Tarana'* which became very popular in India . For this reason Netaji Subhas Chandra Bose decorated Captain Ram Singh with 'Netaji Gold Medal'. He was also presented with one violin and a saxophone by Subhas Chandra Bose.

After the end of the war a large number of INA soldiers surrendered to the British Indian army who were estimated to be 16,000 in number. These rebel soldiers of the Indian army were shipped back to India by July 1944 and put under trial by the Court Martial. Accordingly, they were interrogated, investigated and tried at the Red Fort of Delhi. In the trial, those who were found innocent were acquitted and restored to their original posts; those who joined the INA with somebody's pressure were treated with mercy but dismissed and let off ; and those who willingly joined the INA with the intention of overthrowing the British Government were awarded punishment of various degrees according to severity of offence. Some were imprisoned and some were sentenced to death. Two Gorkha soldiers, viz., Durga Malla and Dal Bahadur Thapa were hanged to death. Captain Ram Singh Thakuri, Dilman Thapa, Chandra Bir Gurung and many others were dismissed from service.

After India's independence in 1947, Captain Ram Singh

Thakuri was re-employed in the Third Battalion of the Uttar Pradesh Police Constabulary and was posted in Lucknow district in 1948. He worked as the Police Band Master in the rank of Inspector till he retired in 1974. While he was serving in the police department he was awarded Governor's Gold Medal in 1956, and President's Police Medal in 1972. After his retirement he received the Uttar Pradesh Sangeet Natak Academy award in 1979 and Mitrasen Award from the Sikkim Government in 1993 and also the Azad Hind Fouz Award from the West Bengal Government in 1996. He died in April 15, 2002 at the ripe age of 88 years. He will be remembered by the country as one of the freedom fighters of India. His marching sing — *'kadam, Kadam badhaye ja,* will ever immortalise his name.'

Kadam kadam badhaye ja
Khusi ke geet gaye ja
Yeh zindagi hai kaum ki
Tu kaum pe lutaye ja

Shere Hind ange lash
Tu maut se kahhi na dar
Jo samne tere aaye
Tu khaak me mitaye ja

Composed and sung by Captain Ram Singh Thakuri for Azad Hind Fauz.

9

Freedom Fighter Bhakta Bahadur Pradhan

Bhakta Bahadur Pradhan was the third generation India born, after his grand-father, Bhim Narayan Pradhan came from Nepal and settled down at Tindharia, district of Darjeeling. His father Jit Bahadur Pradhan, when came of age, left Tindharia in 1890 in search of greener pasture and landed at Sadiya, the eastern-most district of Assam. There the land was plenty, but population was thin and the Government of Assam encouraged Gorkhas from Nepal to settle down in Assam and till the land. Jit Bahadur acquired land, took to agriculture and animal husbandry and established himself well. He also got a son, Bhakta Bahadur at Sadiya on March 28, 1901. But that did not satisfy him for he wanted to take the advantage of the opportunities offered by the time. During those days infrastructural development was taking place in the whole of Upper Assam. The first ever Tea Garden of Assam was established in 1837 at Chabua 28 Km. from Dibrugarh and many more tea gardens were coming up in Assam ; the Assam Oil Company had started drilling and refining oil at Digboi ; mining of coal had begun at Lidu and a new Railway line connecting Lidu and Dibrugarh with rest of Assam had also started. There was, thus, plenty of job opportunities and high demand for men of enterprise and hard work like Jit Bahadur Pradhan. Thus, he moved with his family from Sadiya to Dibrugarh to try his luck. Initially he got himself into a job under the Oil Company and thereafter he struck a deal with the Oil Company for supply of coolies (labours) from Northern Bengal. The Assam Oil Company and the Lidu Mining Company needed large number of coolies to work in its ever expanding factories while the local Assamese people were loath to do labour work. In Northern Bengal,

Rajabhatkhowa, Jalpaiguri, Dooars areas good number of strong, stout and loyal Gorkha coolies were available at cheap wages. Jit Bahadur Pradhan undertook the contract of supplying these labours to the Company on regular basis. The stipulations of the contract were— working period shall be one year minimum, every adult person would get Rs. 16 per month, women Rs. 8 per month and boys from Rs. 8 to Rs. 12 per month. This work of supplying labour was seasonal and most of the time Jit Bahadur had to remain idle. therefore, he worked, side by side, as revenue collector for the Company on commission basis and earned good money.

In these days there was no proper schooling facilities for children at Digboi and hence Jit Bahadur sent his son Bhakta Bahadur to Kurseong Lower Primary School. After he completed Lower Primary standard Bhakta Bahadur was shifted to Tindhare Middle English School. Bhakta Bahadur's academic life was, however, cut off after M.E. School due to some unavoidable reasons.

While he was at Darjeeling, one day Bhakta Bahadur happened to hear the lectures of Desh Bandhu Chitta Ranjan Das, the noted political leader of West Bengal. He did not understand what the great leader said but his personality and forceful language greatly impacted the tender heart of Bhakta Bahadur. In his innermost mind he longed to become like Chitta Ranjan and work for the welfare of the country when he grew up. The two words repeatedly uttered by Chitta Ranjan Das that he could understand were *shoshan* (exploitation) and *utpidran* (oppression) and they hurt his sentiment and roused his hatred against the British.

When he was about sixteen years of age he learnt motor driving by the favour of the General Manager of Assam Oil Company who allowed him to use his car in learning. One fine morning Mr. Flaming, the General Manager took him to the tailor and got his uniform stitched. From the very next day Bhakta Bahadur began to drive the Manager's car in uniform as an appointed driver. Bhakta Bahadur also learnt motor mechanic out of his own inborn ideas for he had great flair in handling mechanical objects. Knowing about his extraordinary capacity in mechanical engineering, the General Manager shifted him from motor driving to the refinery engineering section. After successful completion of five years apprentice course in Refinery Engineering Bhakta

Bhahdur Pradhan was promoted to the post of Refinery Foreman. That was a great lift on the part of a person who had very little background in mechanical engineering.

But his mind was more on politics than on his profession nor did he least bothered for his own personal gain. He was all for the welfare of the country. In 1926, for the first time Mahatma Gandhi came to Guwahati to attend the general conference of the Congress held at Pandu. Many people from Digboi went to Pandu to attend the conference. Bhakta Bahadur also went along with them to see Mahatma Gandhi out of curiosity. Mahatma Gandhi, in his speech said — "we should be self-sufficient in food and clothing ; exploitation should be stopped and freedom must be obtained through non-violence". These words greatly influenced Bhakta Bahadur's mind and he firmly resolved that he must follow what Mahatma Gandhi said. Immediately after coming back to Digboi he enrolled himself as a member of the Congress. From 1934, he started taking active part in Congress Party works. During day time he worked in the refinery factory and by night he used to go out clandestinely for enrolment of Congress members.

In 1937 Pandit Jawaharlal Nehru visited Digboi. A public meeting was held at Jubilee field where Bhakta Bahadur Pradhan took active part as Congress volunteer. Pandit Jawaharlal Nehru's speech inspired the Congress volunteers. He advised them to form Oil Company Workers Union for the unity and solidarity of the workers and for looking after their rights and privileges. After the meeting was over the Officer-in-Charge of Digboi Police Station accosted Bhakta Bahadur Pradhan and took down his identity. A couple of days later, Bhakta Bahadur received a notice from Mr. Ganning,the Deputy Commissioner of north Lakhimpur, prohibiting Bhakta Bahadur Pradhan from entering into an area comprising of one mile radius from the Digboi Railway Station, failing which he would be punished with imprisonment for six months. This, however, did not deter Bhakta Bahadur from carrying out his normal party activities.

After a few days of Pandit Nehru's departure from Digboi, for the first time, there appeared a Workers Union by the name 'Digboi Oil Company Labour Union'. Gradually, the company workers became conscious about their rights and privileges for better housing, better health and sanitation, education for their children and other amenities of life. They became members of the Union and brought about unity and solidarity among themselves. Within a few months the Union grew from strength to strength and its enrolment reached the mark of 10,000. The news of this development caused a great concern to the company management. They started the policy of repression and suppression over the workers individually and collectively through both legal and illegal means. Many workers were threatened stern action, some were suspended and yet others were discharged from the service.

In the wake of brutal suppression perpetrated by the Oil Company management over the Union workers, two innocent employees of the company were dismissed from services without any fault. The Union demanded immediate and unconditional reinstatement of these two employees failing which the Union decided to resort to general strike. The company management took arrogant stance and refused to cancel dismissal notices. This apart, the Government tightened security measures by pressing into service the Assam Rifles from Sadiya. Under this tense situation the Union took out a procession, that shouted slogans and demanded reinstatement of the two discharged employees. To disperse the demonstrators police first resorted to lathi charge and then opened fire on the innocent demonstrators killing, on spot, two persons viz, Praneswar Choudhury and Satyen Chakravarty. That was the first and the biggest demonstration held by the Company Workers Union at Digboi.

The Company Management had kept strict vigilance over the activities of the Union workers while the Deputy Commissioner deployed police and C.I.D. personnel in order to tract down the movements of the Union leaders. One day Bhakta Bahadur Pradhan was coming out from the Labour Union meeting in his car No. ASL 1115 when he was arrested and his car was seized by the police. He was produced before the Magistrate and after a short hearing he was sentenced to one year's rigorous imprisonment. In the jail Bhakta Bahadur found that the food supplied to the inmates of the jail was substandard and unfit for human consumption. He and eleven other inmates of the jail started hunger strike demanding immediate improvement of foodstuff for all prisoners. After three days of hunger strike the participants in the strike reduced from twelve to five members : they were —

Priya Nath Baruah, Harnam Singh, one Pujari .... and Bhakta Bahadur. But they continued the hunger strike until the Inspector General of Police came from Shillong and after carrying out personal inspection of the general condition of jail and the foodstuff he ordered drastic improvement of the food condition.

In the jail, Bhakta Bahadur Pradhan met many political leaders of Assam like Prafulla Goswami, Fatik Chandra Talukdar, Cheniram Dutta, Deben Kakati, Kashiram Deka, etc. They became very close friends and discussed many aspects of their political problems and prepared future plan of action. Another Gorkha leader Dalbirsingh Lohar was also brought to the jail after some months who was a jolly good friend to all and entertained everyone with Bihu *geet* and Nepali *Jhyaure* dance. In this way Bhakta Bahadur passed eleven months in the jail after which he was released.

In 1939 the cloud of Second World War gathered round the horizon. The British dragged India into the war and in 1941 the Japanese brought the war at the doors of Kohima and Imphal. Government of India promulgated the Defence of India Act to detect and deport suspected foreigners out of India. The Digboi Assam Oil Company falsely implicated Bhakta Bahadur Pradhan under the provisions of the Defence of India Rules and he was ordered not to be, within 72 hours of the receipt of the order, in any place within the district of Lakhimpur, Sibsagar, Darrang, Nowgong and Kamrup districts. (Appendix-IV). That was a devastating order effecting not only the personal life of Bhakta Bahadur but also the lives of his family and children for indefinite period of time. Accordingly Bhakta Bahadur left his family under the care of his father Jit Bahadur Pradhan and travelled aimlessly around the other districts of Assam and outside Assam without any purpose. He went to Tripura, Calcutta, Purnia, Bhagalpur, Darjeeling, Gauwahati, Tezpur, etc., sometimes under the guise of a *sadhu* and at times as political leader and at others as just a traveller. The mental suffering that he had undergone and the agonies he suffered during these days were better to be guessed rather than described.

After long six years of his banishment from Digboi, in 1947 India got freedom when the British left India and their order of externation ceased to hold good. Bhakta Bahadur Pradhan heaved a sigh of relief as his torture and hardship came to an end. He returned home and joined his family and children. Digboi unrolled red carpet for him. The Dibrugarh Pradesh Congress Committee offered him ceremonial greetings and a certificate of Class I Political Sufferer Appendix V. Sarat Chandra Sinha, the Chief Minister of Assam offered him a *Copper Plate* (*Tamrapatra*) in recognition of his supreme sacrifice that he made for the freedom of India and for the Oil Company workers.

This is an unvarnished and untold story of an ordinary but a man of high ideals, Bhakta Bahadur Pradhan.

10

Freedom Fighter Bishnulal Upadhyaya

Bishnulal Upadhyaya was born on the 16th July, 1917 at Majhgoan in a middle class Nepali family and was the second among the five sons. His father Brihaspati Upadhyaya was a professional grazier who had a large herd of cows and buffaloes in his farm at Kajiranga.. Bishnulal was by nature a mild and sober boy whose childhood was uneventful like those of average boys of his locality. His father put him in the local Hatibandha Middle Combined School for his early education wherefrom he successfully passed out in 1934. He was married at an early age of fifteen years while still in Middle school with one of his school mate named Annapurna Devi. After completion of Middle school he was sent to the Government High School at Tezpur where he lived in the house of one Khadananda Adhikari at Nepali Patti. In 1938 he passed Matriculation in first division and got himself admitted in the Cotton College, Guahati for higher study. While studying in Cotton College he joined freedom movement of India together with other fellow students. In the wake of Quit India movement of 1942 the teachers and students were actively involved in the movement and all schools and colleges were closed indefinitely. Bishnulal came home and took active part in organizing freedom movement. As a young man he derived inspiration from the prominent Congress leaders like Omio Kumar Das, Gahan Chandra Goswami, Vijoy Chandra Bhagavati, Chhabilal Upadhyaya, Bogiram Saikia, etc., and organized peoples' rallies and demonstrations against the British rule. He played an active role in the historic demonstration of 20 September, 1942 that succeeded in pulling down British Union Jack and hoisting of Congress flag at Behali Police Station building. On that day many

Congress leaders were arrested including Bishnulal Upadhyaya and imprisoned at Tezpur jail. Knowing Bisnulal to be a third year B.A. student of Cotton College, the Magistrate, before pronouncing his judgment told him, – "You are a young student ; you have a future ; besides that, you belong to the backward Nepali community ; if you agree to sign a bond stating that you did not know what you did and that you would not do such act in future, I would set you free". Bishnulal replied — " I did it knowing fully well and I will continue to do the same". Hearing such a drastic reply of Bishnulal the Magistrate sentenced him to six months rigorous imprisonment.

In 1943 after the political movement was concluded he resumed his study in Cotton College as a third year student and after one year in 1944 he passed his Graduation with Honours in Sanskrit. Earlier on 31 August, 1943 Bishnulal had been appointed as the Head Master of Behali High School in order to fill the vacancy that was caused due to resignation submitted by Anandeswar Baruah. Accordingly, immediately after his graduation he resumed his post as Head Master of the said school. He worked in that School for a long period of fourteen years until in 1957 when he was offered a Congress ticket to contest election to the Assam Legislative Assembly.

During his long stint as the Head Master of the Behali High school he made a great contribution towards education among the backward people besides bringing about manifold improvements to the school itself. He was a great teacher himself. He not only taught but also inspired his students. An eminent educationist said, — "There are four kinds of teachers ; some read out, some simply talk, some explain and some inspire". Bishnulal Upadhyaya belonged to the last category of teachers.

His involvement in active politics began since 1950s when he became the member of the Tezpur Local Board with Congress ticket. In 1957, for the first time, he won the election and became the member of the Assam Legislative Assembly from Gahapur constituency and thereafter he continued to remain in that office for three terms consecutively till 1972. After a break of five years he became Congress MLA once again from Behali constituency for one full term from 1978 till 1983. Thus he worked as member of the Assam Legislative Assembly for a period of twenty years.

(four full terms) and turned out to be a veteran Congress leader. As a parliamentarian Bishnulal Upadhyaya was an upright democrat. He was strictly guided by democratic principles and actively participated in debates in the Assembly. He often brought before the house for discussion important issues concerning the State and helped arriving at constructive decisions. He put up Assembly Questions to draw Government attention on the problems experienced by the people of various walks of life and tried to address those issues.

He was imbued with Gandhian ideology and tried to follow the principles of Mahatma Gandhi in letter and spirit. He wore snow-white Khadi Kurta and dhoti and within his mortal frame was a fine sensitive mind, a rare delicacy of feeling and a large generous impulse towards those who are deprived. In 1960 when Binoba Bhave visited Assam Bishnulal became one of the active members of the Assam State Binoba Bhave Reception Committee. He also acted as the Chairman of the two-day seminar held at Helem Revenue Circle office on 13-14 October, 1966 for the review of the Assam Bhudan Act. It was because of his active participation in the Bhudan movement that many landless cultivators of Helem Revenue Circle were benefited with lands. Among those who played active role in the Bhudan movement were Srimati Amal Prabha Das, Sakuntala Choudhury, Hem Bharali, Rampada Pathak and others.

During the twenty years of his stint as MLA. the State of Assam faced a number of turbulent situations of which Assamese Language Bill, Oil Refinery movement and influx of outsiders in Assam were the most disturbing ones. The agitation launched by the AASU and *AAGSP against outsiders* (Non-Assamiya) rocked whole of Assam which took a toll of several thousands human lives. The foreigners movement of 1979-85 destabilized the very parliamentary process and the Government administration of Assam, so much so that, for the first time the State came under Presidential rule. Never before had the Assam Legislative Assembly experienced such defections by its members. In such a trying situation Bishnulal Upadhyaya remained a loyal and firm parliamentarian and tried his best to restore peace and tranquillity giving moral support to the victims of the Assam agitation. He rose to the occasion to provide moral support to the thousands of

Nepali families who fell victims to the senseless violence and were rendered homeless during the Assam movement. Through the press and platform he tried to justify the case of Nepalis living permanently in Assam. He wrote articles in the newspapers and spoke in the floor of the Assembly about the atrocities perpetrated to the Nepalis. He led a number of delegations of Nepali leaders to wait upon the Chief Minister and the Governor of Assam and pleaded for the political rights and legal protection of the Nepalis of the North East who were the genuine citizens of India. As the President of Assam Gorkha Sammelan, he also met Atal Behari Bajpai, the Prime Minister of India, and urged upon him for amendment of the Article 7 of the Peace and Friendship Treaty 1950 between India and Nepal so as to stop free passage of Nepalese nationals into India, which according to the Assam Gorkha Sammelan, was the main cause of irritation leading to the agitation against the Nepalis of Assam.

Bishnulal Upadhyaya played leading role in socio-political organizations among the Nepalis in the entire North East India. He acted as the General Secretary of the All India Gorkha League, Assam Branch in 1947. After the All India Gorkha League was dissolved and Assam Gorkha Sammelan was established in 1966 he became its Vice-President and in 1969 he took over as the President in which post he remained till 1982. It was during this period of time that the Assam Gorkha Sammelon expanded itself into 106 branches all over Assam and did the maximum socio-cultural works under his able leadership. The publication of Bulletin, the mouth-piece of the Assam Gorkha Sammelan was started during his time, which helped establish better link between the branches and generate of political awareness among the Nepalis of Assam.

The officials of the Government of Assam attempted to deny the voting rights to Nepalis on several occasion when Bishnulal Upadhyaya took up the matter with the Chief Minister for withdrawal of such restrictions. In 1960 the Deputy Commissioner of Garo Hills by his letter No. GE 72/60/5 dated 2nd September, 1960 ordered that the Nepalis have to first obtain Indian citizenship certificates before their names were included in the Voter Lists failing which their names if already included in the Voter Lists of 1952/1957 would also be struck out. That order of the Deputy

Commissioner caused a commotion among the Nepalis residing for generations in Assam. Bishnulal Upadhyaya not only took up the matter with the Chief Minister of Assam but also raised the issue in the Assam Legislative Assembly and compelled the Government to instruct all Deputy Commissioners and Sub-Divisional Officers to include the names of the Nepalis as voters on the basis of Revenue documents (Patta) and other proofs of permanent residence.

Again in 1970 Lok Sabha election a large number of Nepalis of Dibrugarh, Sadiya, Chaoakhowa, Chunpura, Dhoula, Jonai villages were not allowed to vote by the Presiding Officers on the ground that their names were struck out with red ink. Bishnulal Upadhyaya through Assembly Starred Question No. 688 dated 25-5-1971 asked the Government on what basis the names of the said voters were cancelled from the Voter Lists. The matter was enquired by a Special Enquiry Commission and finally 3500 Nepalis names were restored back into the Voter Lists.

In October, 1979 Shri R.N. Mathur, Superintendent of Police, district Lakhimpur, Assam served notices to twenty Nepali families of Bihpuria village to leave India within a period of two weeks from the date of the notice and not to re-enter India again. The news created a sensation, fear psychosis and a sense of insecurity among the Indian Nepalis at large. A deputation of the Assam Gorkha Sammelan, consisting of four MLAs including Bishnulal Upadhyaya waited upon the Chief Minister of Assam and the Leader of the Assam Legislature Party, Shri Sarat Chandra Sinha who expressed surprise at the uncalled for action of the concerned officer. The Chief Minister immediately darted a wireless message instructing the Superintendent of Police to stop further action on the matter until Government orders Realising his mistake the Police Officer hurriedly called back all the copies of the notices issued by him from the villagers.

Bishnulal Upadhyaya worked not only for the Nepalis but also served the general interest of greater Assam and worked for the benefit of people of all castes, communities and religions. He believed in social harmony and equal opportunities for all and to that end he eagerly tried to establish a rapport with all classes of people. He worked for the welfare of Assamese culture and language and participated in various Assamese social functions like Bihu festivals, Rash Mela, Sankardev Tithi, etc. He was actively involved in Asom Sahitya Sabha as a life member of the same. He wrote books and articles in Assamese language and enriched Assamese literature. Dr. Jogendra Narayan Bhuyan, Maheswar Neog and Satish Chandra Kakati praised Bishnulal Upadhyaya as an accomplished Assamese writer. His book in Assamese— *Dugaraaki Mahaan Bibhuti,* in which he portrayed the lives of Assamese Prophet Sankardev and Nepali Epic Poet Bhanukhakta, he tried to build a golden bridge between the Assamese and the Nepali people and their culture and religion. His another Assamese book — *Eri Ahaa Din Bor,* would go a long way to keep his multi-faceted personality evergreen in the hearts of Assamese people — said Dr. Jogendra Narayan Bhuyan. He was awarded Phulchand Khandelwal award by Asom Sahitya Sabha in recognition of his valuable contribution to literature. Addressing the meeting held on 27 September, 2003 at Golaghat organised by the Golaghat Branch of the Asom Sahitya Sabha for handing over the Phulchand Khandelwal award to him, Bishnulal Upadhyaya said — " The satisfaction which I did not get from my involvement in politics as a member of the Legislative Assembly for four consecutive terms, I had that through my literary career of the last eighteen years. Because I have realized the truth that the modern politics breaks the nation while literature builds it up".

Bishnulal Upadhyaya was a connoisseur in Nepali literature and occupied a place among the high ranking Nepali literateurs. He was a prolific writer and wrote as many as seventeen books of which twelve are in Nepali and the rest are in Assamese. In reply to a question put up by a journalist he said – "Literature affords an opportunity to come closer to the masses. That is why I prefer to serve the people through literature rather than politics". His penetrating and intuitive faculty in writing and his logical coherence and candid language made it easy for him to reach to the depth of his readers hearts. I have no doubt in mind that had he not joined politics which took away twenty years of his precious life he would have turned out to be a famous writer.

11

Freedom Fighter Chhabilal Upadhyaya

Babu Chhabilal Upadhyaya's father Kashinath Upadhyaya who hailed from Irautar village of Nepal towards 1874/75 and settled down at Budigang about ten Km from Biswanath Charali, district Sonitpur. While living at Budigang three sons were born to Kashinath Upadhyaya who were named as Bhimlal, Chhabilal and Ramlal respectively. Chhabilal was born on 12 May, 1882. After a few years Kashinath shifted from Budigang to Majgoan (also known as Gangmouthan) where he was blessed with two more sons who were named as Hari Prasad and Bishnulal.

The village (Gangmouthan) was situated a couple of Km north of the famous river Brahmaputra that intervened Kajiranga reserved forest, the present Game sanctuary, renowned for its one-horned rhinoceros. Majgoan and Nakunia were two adjacent Nepali villages which were flanked by two big Assamese villages named Bansbari and Hatibandha, to the south-east and to the north-east of Majgoan respectively.

In those days the people were extremely backward in education and villages were devoid of educational institutions. Except the distantly located two Lower Primary Schools — one at Jhalukbari and the other at Hatibandha villages — there were no other school in the whole area of Mouja Behali. Although Chhabilal was sent to the Hatibandha L.P. School he had to end up his academic life at the primary level. But he was a studious boy and he read story books, novels, magazines and on whatever he could lay his hand. By the time he attained his adulthood he had acquired good knowledge from the books of Bamkim Chandra, Sarat Chandra, Raja Ram Mohan Roy, Swami Vivekananda, etc. He used to read news papers and magazines like *Ananda Bazar Patrika, Basumati,* etc., and update his knowledge about the happenings in the country. Reading and reciting by heart the *slokas* of the *Ramayana* and *Mahabharata* were like singing Hindi film songs by our youths today. Swimming and boating in Brahmaputra river, catching wood-logs during summer floodings and searching of tortoise eggs in winter were some of the youthful pastimes of Chhabilal. Hunting deer and capturing deer cubs were other games that fascinated young Chhabilal. With a hefty well-built body and tremendous courage and will-power within, he was a man of natural command and of leadership.

The political and nationalistic consciousness of Babu Chhabilal Upadhyaya was, however, triggered by an incident that took place in 1920 when, on one fateful day a battery of Forest officials, accompanied by armed police arrived at the scene, and set fire on the cattlesheds and dwelling houses of Nepali graziers of Kajiranga numbering hundreds of families. Within minutes, the entire dwelling houses and cattlesheds, the household goods and wearing apparels turned into heaps of ashes. The greatest damage was suffered by Chhabilal Upadhyaya as his establishments were the biggest among the Nepali graziers. No prior notice was served, nor a reasonable time was allowed to them to salvage their household goods. These Nepali graziers had been living there peacefully for more than fifty years paying grazing fees to the Government at stipulated rates per head of cattle. Such an unjust and inhuman act of the British Government mortally hurt the sentiment of loyal Chhabilal. He became disillusioned and rebellious and looked for a course of action that would provide the graziers with collective safety and security of life and property. Finally they decided to come under the banner of the political organization under the leadership of Chhabilal Upadhyaya, Advocate Chandranath Sarma, Ramlal Upadhyaya, Bogiram Saikia, Hari Prasad Upadhyaya, etc.

The golden opportunity came his way when Babu Chhabilal Upadhyaya was invited to preside over a meeting of the Assam Association. The historic meeting of the 'Assam Association' held at Jorhat on 17th April, 1921 marked the turning point of the life of Babu Chhabilal Upadhyaya. The meeting adopted historic decision to merge the 'Assam Association' with All India Congress Committee and to launch non-cooperation movement of Mahatma

Gandhi in a stronger and wider parameter. The meeting also decided to bring the Gorkhas of Assam under the fold of the Congress and to take up the issue of Kajiranga eviction of graziers with the Government of Assam. The Gorkhas joined the National Congress under the leadership of Babu Chhabilal Upadhyaya, and Assamese leaders like Tarunram Phukan, Nabin Chandra Bardoloi, Dr. Hem Chandra Baruah, Amiya Kumar Das, Kuladhar Chaliha, Gopinath Bordoloi, etc. The Gorkhas actively took part in the non-cooperation movement of 1921 protesting against the repressive measures adopted by government. The news of heinous killing of hundreds of innocent people at Jallianwala Bagh on 13 April,1919 brought a deep sense of indignation and anguish in the young heart of Chhabilal. In retaliation, he together with his followers boycotted foreign clothes, used home woven clothes, helped collection of Tilak Swaraj Fund, boycotted offices, schools and colleges.

Babu Chhabilal Upadhyaya was a real Gandhian leader with Khadi kurta and knee-length dhoti. He accepted the doctrine of non-violence of Mahatma Gandhi as axiom. Gandhiji said, "I believe that non-violence is infinitely superior to violence, forgiveness is more manly than punishment : Forgiveness is the ornament of the hero and it adorns a soldier" (Jawaharlal Nehru: *Autobiography*, 1936, p. 83). He took the leadership of the Nepali community of Assam during non-co-operation movement of Mahatma Gandhi in 1921. He reached every home meeting and inducing them to part with foreign clothes and to burn them in public meetings. He was very practical man and proved before people that he literally practised the old adage — "Example is better than precept". According to an anecdote, Chhabilal Babu's wife was in possession of many expensive foreign clothes of which she agreed to give away all but one piece of which she begged of him to spare. She pleaded that if she would retain one piece of cloth no great harm would befall. At this Babu Chhabilal retorted back saying — "You foolish woman, don't you see, if one drop of *chuk* (citric acid) fell off in a pail of milk, wouldn't the whole milk get spoiled? So also with one piece of foreign cloth the entire mission would fail." Unfortunately for Mrs. Upadhyaya, the first cloth that was thrown into the bonfire was that of her choicest one. For, Babu Chhabilal said — "Charity begins at home".

Mahatma Gandhi also faced with similar experience once when he proposed to donate all the valuable gifts received by him to a Trust which Kasturbaji objected. She agreed to part with them only after Gandhiji sternly prevailed upon her.

True to Gandhiji's ideals, Babu Chhabilal Upadhyaya introduced *Sutra-Yagnya* at various villages and induced women folk to undertake spinning and weaving *khadi* cloth in whole of Behali Mouja. He introduced *Madhuvani Charkha* (Spinning – Wheel) and improved handloom and made them available to intending weavers at subsidized prices. He made it a system to begin every gathering or meeting by *Sutra-Yagnya*, or spinning session which practice remained in his locality for a long time. Wearing of khadi clothes became a symbol of patriotism and respect. He himself never wear other than short *khadi dhoti* and *kurta*, but seldom puton Gandhi cap, for reasons best known to himself.

Another significant feature of Gandhiji's reforms that Babu Chhabilal Upadhyaya avidly followed was boycott of alcohol, opium ganja and other products injurious to health. This movement had two—fold effects — one, it saves lakhs of poor people of India from the ruin of their health and economy; and two, it prevents British from earning excise tax by selling these harmful products. In those days the government used to issue *pattas* (licences) to people for buying opium, alcohol, ganja, etc., from government authorized vendors who had to pay certain stipulated exise duties to the government.

Because of his involvement in all these anti-government activities the police intelligence were always after Babu Chhabilal and the Deputy Commissioner was closely monitoring his movements. One fine morning the police came to his house and seized his double-barrel gun and a revolver. He was also served with a notice signed by the Deputy Commissioner, Darrang district that if he did not stop *satyagraha* movement forthwith he would be banished from India. But he did not pay any heed to the notification of the D.C. Babu Chhabilal Upadhyaya not only loved India as his own country but also was a real patriot This fact is borne out by the following episode that took place in his life.

In 1921, a public meeting was held at Tezpur Polo-field in connection with according befitting welcome to Mahatma Gandhi who was to arrive at Tezpur for the first time. Babu Chhabilal Upadhyaya was actively organising the proceedings of the meeting. The Superintendent of Police, Tezpur who was around the corner spying the activities of the Congress workers, accosted Babu Chhabilal after the meeting was over and took him in his car to some secluded place. Trying to dissuade Babu Chhabilal from participating in the Congress movement, the Superintendent of Police said — "Mr. Chhabilal, you are from Nepal which is already an independent country. Why do you join the Congress and go against the Government of India ? Please stop doing this meaningless thing , I would release your seized gun and revolver and also I would do anything you want me to do for you and your Gorkha people if you refrain from Congress movement". To this Chhabilal replied — " Well, Nepal might be an independent country, that does not matter to me. What matters me is Assam. I am born and brought up in Assam and I would also die in Assam. Assam is my birth place and India is my country. So the problem of India is my problem and the political movement of India is my movement. Therefore, I cannot remain aloof from this" Mr. Superintendent of Police, dropped Chhabilal from his vehicle without a single word and speeded away.

In the evening when this episode was told to Mahatma Gandhi during his chit-chat in the house of Paramananda Agarwal at Tezpur Gandhiji expressed happiness and said — "Well done Chhabilalji".

Babu Chhabilal was greatly inspired by Mahatma Gandhi during his talk with him and he devoted more time in the party's work as active Congress worker. He was elected one of the delegates to attend the Congress Working Committee to be held in Ahmedabad in 1921. But he could not attend that meeting as he was arrested on the same day and put in Tezpur jail together with his brother Hari Prasad Upadhyaya who was helping him in his works.

After two months in jail, one day Mr. B.C. Allen, the Commissioner for Assam Valley came to the jail and requested Babu Chhabilal to change his political stance and to give up Congress movement. He also assured Babu Chhabilal that if he had any personal problem then he would be glad to offer any assistance that he might need from him. But Babu Chhabilal was not a person to be inveigled so easily. He replied humbly —"Sir, I have no personal problem as such. I am working for my country and my interest cannot be greater than my country's interest'. The Commissioner could very well understand his mind. He left the jail with vengeance and the next day he enhanced the jail term of Babu Chhabilal from four to six months. In the jail Babu Chhabilal had the opportunity of meeting many political leaders and after the completion of his jail period when he returned home he was a different man — a man with wider knowledge and experience of Indian political movement.

As a leader of the Gorkhas settled in Assam and in the surrounding Hill districts of Assam, Babu Chhabilal stood always for the protection of their rights and privileges. Under the Government of India Act 1935, Provincial Autonomy was granted to the people of India. In all Provincial Legislative Assemblies the members were directly elected by the people through casting of votes. In Assam there was a bicameral Legislature consisting of Legislative Council and Legislative Assembly. In the year 1935 the first general election was held to elect members to these Legislative bodies in which the Gorkhas permanently living in Assam were also given the right of franchise like any other inhabitants of Assam. But the next year the question of Indian citizenship was raised by the Government and the Gorkhas were debarred from exercising the right to vote. The Government of India, through a notification stated that the Gorkhas living in India had first to obtain certificates of becoming the subjects of the British India before they would be allowed the right to vote. The above decision of the government not only questioned the voting rights, but also involved many other socio-economic rights and privileges of the Gorkhas which might have far reaching consequences in course of time. This was, straight way a grave injustice meted out to the Gorkhas who had their domicile by virtue of living in India for generations. Babu Chhabilal Upadhyaya was a far sighted politician and he took up this matter immediately with the government at various levels. He sent memoranda to the Governor General of India, the Prime Minister of Assam (during colonial regime he was designated as such) and the Governor of Assam. He personally met Sir Syid Sahdulla, the Prime Minister of Assam and pleaded for the right of franchise of the Gorkhas. Nothing positive, however, followed for months together until Sir Rohini Kumar Choudhury, the

Revenue Minister of Assam, intervened with the impugned Government notification on the legitimate ground that a domiciled citizen connot be denied the right of franchise. So, eventually the government agreed to give voting rights to Gorkhas provided that they prove their domicile in India with substantial evidence. The government, therefore, decided that the Gorkhas who possessed land revenue Periodic Pattas would be eligible to cast their votes.

Babu Chhabilal Upadhyaya was always the forerunner in social welfare works. He realized the role of education in the development of the country and, therefore, he took active part in spreading education among the people of Behali Mouja. As we have already mentioned, there were only two Primary schools in the whole of Behali Mouja. He took up with the government to upgrade the Hatibandha L.P. School into Middle Vernacular school in 1927 and later on converted it into Middle English school. He was also responsible for establishing one Theatre Hall at Majgoan for the recreation of the people as well as development of Nepali art and culture. The Theatre Hall was one of the best in Assam of those days and comparable to the noted Bana-stage and Bengali Theatre Hall of Tezpur town.

It was also with his relentless hard work and resolution of missionary zeal that he was able to establish a High School at Majgoan in 1939 which he named as Behali High English school. The school was initially started in the Majgoan Theatre Hall and subsequently was shifted to nearby Hatibandha Grazing field around 1948. Babu Chhabilal went door to door with begging bowl for collecting fund for the school. In this respect he can be called Madon Mohan Malaviya who collected bricks after bricks from people for construction of the Banares Hindu University. In those days rupees five hundred was equivalent to fifty thousand rupees and those few generous gentlemen who donated five hundred rupees or more, their enlarged photographs were hung on the walls of the school office room. I was a student of this school from class four up to Matriculation and I used to see those photos and read the names of the rich donors. Some of these names were — Govindaram Upadhyaya, Khadananda Upadhyaya, Gangadhar Upadhyaya, Mulkraj Sukla, Bogiram Saikia, Tikaram Upadhyaya, etc.

In the wake of the Second World War the political situation of

India became fluid. The rising cost of articles including daily necessities of life adversely affected the life of the Indian people. Most of the Congress leaders including Subhas Chandra Bose and Raja Gopalachari were annoyed with the Indian Government for dragging India into the war. The refugees from Burma proved already heavy burden on the people of Assam and Bengal. The Japanese brought the war to the door step of India's north-east. Even Mahatma Gandhi who supported British during the first World War, wrote in the *Harijan* — "The presence of the British in India is an invitation to the Japanese to invade India". In such situation the Congress Working Committee held at Lahore adopted resolution to step up the freedom movement by demanding full independence (*Purna-swaraj*). The All India Congress Committee held at Bombay on August 8, 1942 ratified the resolution. Thus Mahatma Gandhi declared "Quit India Movement" from that day. However, the Government reacted and it swiftly. The very next day, on August 9, all the members of the Congress Working Committee including Gandhiji were arrested at early dawn before they woke up from bed and the Congress Party was declared illegal organization The other political leaders of the provinces were also arrested one by one. From Behali Mouja Babu Chhabilal Upadhyaya, Hari Prasad Upadhyaya, Bogiram Saikia and many others were imprisoned. From Dibrugarh Dalbirsingh Lohar, Bhakta Bahadur Pradhan and other Assamese leaders were also arrested and put in jail. The peoples agitation flared up everywhere in India. In Behali the teachers, students and the public took out a processions on the 20 September, leading to the Police Station shouting slogans, *"inquilab zindabad"*, *"bandemataram"*, *"karenge yaa marenge"* The processionists marched into the Thana compound in complete disregard of the police barricades. One of the volunteers climbed the ladder, reached up to the roof of the Thana building and unfurled the Tricolour Congress flag. Sukumar Chakravarty, the officer-in-charge of Police Station took out his revolver but could not open fire. After that day police repression and atrocity started upon the Congress volunteers and the members of the Mukti Bahini. Police arrested Kumud Chandra Sarma, Molan Sarma, Bisnulal Upadhyaya, Rabiram Saikia, Sarada Prasanna Dutta and many others. Appreciating the success of the freedom struggle movement of Behali the Asom Bani newspaper, dated 23rd January, 1980 stated — " Large number of Nepalis of

Behali participated in the freedom movement under the able leadership of Shri Chhabilal Upadhyaya which surpassed even the agitations of the Assamese people of many places. This was, really not a mean success of Babu Chhabilal Upadhyaya.

In 1947 the Annual General Conference of the All India Gorkha League was held at Tezpur. On the day of the Open Session more than five thousand Nepalis of Darrang district participated in the procession with Khukuris in hand and carrying banners and posters written — "Thirty lakh khukuris will protect Assam from clubbing it into East Pakistan". This was in opposition against the Two-Nation Theory of Jinna, dividing India into two dominions and clubbing Muslim majority provinces into Pakistan. The massive demonstration by the Nepalis of this dimension was for the first time in Assam and the credit, undoubtedly, would go to Babu Chhabilal's capability of leadership. The book *Political History of Assam* Vol. (III), Published by the government of Assam, writes — "They (Nepalis) supported the mandate of Assam Assembly to the members of the Constituent Assembly from Assam not to sit in section 'C' but to frame a provisional constitution of their own. They joined hands with local people in opposing the demands of 'Pakistan' and declared that if necessary, thirty lakh khukuris would be used to defend the unity of the motherland". This was also one of the major resolutions adopted by the General Conference of the All India Gorkha League in Tezpur Session.

Thus Balu Chhabilal Upadhyaya, pioneer of the poletical movement of Assam, the stalwart of freedom movements and the forebear of the Nepalis of North Eastern frontiers passed away on 25th January, 1980 at the ripe old are of 98 years.

12

Freedom Fighter Dalbirsingh Lohar

Dalbirsingh Lohar was synonymous with a lotus flower that bloomed on a muddy water without the knowledge and care of anyone and that was plucked for the offerings at the altar of God. Nobody was aware of the actual date of birth of Dalbirsingh nor anybody knew about his personal life but he, in his later life, turned out to be a man of towering personality and a great leader. According to one source he was born in 1915, in the same year, Gauri Sankar Bhattacharjee, the noted Communist leader of Assam, was born. He had three elder brothers and one elder sister and he was the youngest among the five siblings. Since his early life he loved helping others and doing social works. He had the attitude of sacrifice and love for the society in complete disregard of his own self. He was mere a boy of fifteen years in 1929 when he joined as Congress volunteer and participated in the movement against the Cunninghum Circular for which he was arrested and jailed for a term of three months. After he was released from jail he left his school and actively participated in the *Satyagraha* movement of Mahatma Gandhi. The one incident that inspired his tender heart was when Mahatma Gandhi visited Dibrugarh in 1921. He, along with other school mates, was made to wear Gandhi cap and was lined up with miniature Congress Flags in hands and then led in a procession to the venue of the meeting where Gandhiji lectured. He did not understand what Gandhiji said about, but what inspired him was the idea of being great man like Mahatma Gandhi and working for the country when he grew up.

Dibrugarh, the home town of Dalbirsingh, was surrounded by many Tea gardens and the Digboi Oil Company was only a few kilometres away from Dibrugarh. Dalbirsingh grew up in the midst of Tea Gardens and the tea garden labourers were his close neighbours. He felt pity for the miserable living conditions of these labourers. Their poverty, hunger, disease and illiteracy made him think over how to get them rid from these social injustices. His mind became rebellious against the Tea garden management which, he thought, was to be blamed for these consequences. His indignation towards the Tea Garden Managers comes out forcefully from the following poem composed by him in Assamese language—

" Where, on earth, you tea garden labour,
Become rich by making your blood water?
As the rain drops fall on your head
Through the thatched roof of your cottage,
You feel like dying, b'cause you gave blood for tea,
Ask for Leave ? No leave even for your baby's death
Failing to attend the duty wou'd get struck
Your name from the roll".

Thus Dalbirsingh Lohar became a grassroot level leader for the tea garden workers, besides being an active freedom fighter. He worked as the President of the Assam Tea Workers Union for a long period of six years and successfully brought about many improvements of basic amenities in the life of the workers. He, however, was not alone in this struggle, there were many other Tea Union leaders who worked with him, such as Sadhu Singh, Beiram Singh, Dr. Vinoy Chakravarty, Nilamani Borphukan and Aziuddin Choudhury.

The Lahore Annual Session of the Congress held on November 29, 1929 elected Jawaharlal Nehru as its President and at the mid-night of December 31, 1929 the Congress Committee declared *Purna Swaraj* as its goal. The Working Committee then authorized Gandhiji to launch a programme of Civil Disobedience with the ultimate aim of attaining complete independence.

Accordingly on March 12, 1930, Mahatma Gandhi started Civil Disobedience Movement by breaking the Salt Law and making salt at the sea beach called Dandi, a small village in Gujarat. On that day, early morning he marched from Sabarmati Ashram on foot with 78 followers and reached the sea at Dandi on April 5 where Gandhiji and his followers made salt in violation of the salt laws. The movement of Civil Disobedience spread all over the country. The wind of the movement reached Assam and Dibrugarh. Dalbirsingh Lohar, Bhakta Bahadur Pradhan and many other Gorkhas joined the movement and broke the laws by observing boycott of foreign goods, withholding payment of government taxes and land revenues etc.

In 1940, the workers of the Digboi Oil Company resorted to strike in order to put pressure on the Oil Company management to fulfil their demands. The Deputy Commissioner of Dibrugarh promulgated section 144 Cr.P.C. prohibiting taking out procession. But Dalbirsingh did not pay any heed and held demonstration in front of the General Manager's office. As a punishment for this Dalbirsingh was externed from Assam and was allowed to live in Goalpara after signing a bond to maintain peace and good behaviour. Dalbirsingh Lohar, however, was not a person to care the bond and remain within Goalpara. He contravened the terms of bond and was imprisoned once again.

The clarion call given by Mahatma Gandhi for non-co-operation movement reached the nooks and corners of Assam. The Gorkhas who had been living in the hills and plains of Assam responded magnificently under the leadership of Dalbir Singh Lohar and Bhakta Bahadur Pradhan of Dibrugarh and Babu Chhabilal Upadhyaya, Hari Prasad Upadhyaya, and Bishnulal Upadhyaya of Tezpur/ Behali. They boycotted foreign clothes, Used Khadi clothes and stopped payment of revenue to Government. Babu Chhabilal Upadhyaya was arrested and imprisoned at Tezpur jail for a term of six months on the charge of joining non-co-operation movement. His brother Hari Prasad Upadhyaya was also imprisoned for three months. Their Double Barrel Guns and revolvers were seized. During this time Dalbr Singh and Bhakta Bahadur Pradhan were also arrested and imprisoned in Dibrugarh jail.

During Quit India Movement in 1942 all top leaders of India including Mahatma Gandhi were arrested and put in jails at different places. The Indian National Congress was declared as illegal organization. The Gorkhas of Assam participated in the Quit India movement and suffered arrest, lathi charge and physical torture. In Dibrugarh a large number of tea garden workers and Gorkhas took out procession defying the promulgation of 144 Cr. P.C. under the leadership of Dalbirsingh Lohar and Bhakta Bahadur Pradhan.

In 1945 election, Dalbirsing Lohar was given Congress nomination to contest from the reserved seat of Lahowal constituency. This seat was reserved for the representation of the Tea garden labourers and persons belonging to certain communities including the 'Lohar' community could contest the election. Thus Dalbirsingh Lohar contested and won the election with the overwhelming support of the Tea garden workers. Besides being an M.L.A, he held the office of the President of the Assam Tea Workers Union and also the Vice-President of the Assam Branch of the Indian National Trade Union Congress (INTUC) for quite a long time. Over and above this he was the Executive Member of the Assam Oil Company Labour Union, and the President of the Assam State Transport Workers Association. He brought about a good number of changes and improvements in the working of the Assam Medical College at Dibrugarh as a member of the Governing Body.

Dalbirsingh Lohar had an imposing personality. With khadi kurta, paijama and khadi Jawahar coat he looked a typical *Congressi Neta*. In the floor of the Assembly he was a good orator in Assamese language. He could give befitting replies to the charges made by the opposition members in the floor of the House and justify the works carried out by the government. Nilamani Phukan, the former President of the Asom Sahitya Sabha said — "Dalbirsingh Lohar could speak better Assamese than me". He had a short and stocky body with a pair of big bulging eyes over his broad face and when he gets lock-horned in debate in the Assembly his two rolling eye-balls virtually emitted fire. He had, however, a soft heart within his stocky body which belied his external appearance. He had special concern for the women and children and for their welfare he established Tea Workers' Welfare Organization at Dibrugarh attached to the Circle Office of the Tea Workers Union in 1956 which is functioning even to this day as one of the best NGOs. He worked as its President till his death in 1969. He also founded a Cultural Unit of the Assam Tea workers Association for the revival and development of the rich tribal culture of the tea workers. This was the first step in this direction taken by the Indian Trade Union Congress. This Cultural Unit organized cultural shows at various tea gardens of Assam and, on many occasions, Dalbirsingh Lohar himself remained present and provided much needed encouragement to the participants. This Cultural Unit contributed greatly in developing and propagating tribal cultures through the medium of stage and the documentary films because of which the tribal *jhumur* dance of the tea garden labourers has become so popular today.

He contested general election in 1952 with Congress ticket and returned to Assam Legislative Assembly for the second time. He was a dynamic leader and was rightly called as – "*Shramik Neta* Dalbirsingh Lohar". It is a tradition in India and for that matter in Assam, to attach sobriquets to the leaders as a token of recognition of their good works, such as – Lokmanya Tilak, Pandit Jawaharlal Nehru, Karmavir Nabin Chandra Bordoloi, Lokapriya Gopinath Bordoloi, etc. No person has ever been able to devote himself with so much of zeal and dedication as Dalbirsingh Lohar did for the cause of the downtrodden Tea garden labourers and the oil company workers. On one occasion he came to attend the Working Committee meeting of the Assam branch of the I.N.T.U.C. in spite of his illness and chaired the meeting lying down on a bench. He could mix up with all walks of people with equal warmth of heart and earnestness. He travelled in third class railway with tea garden labourers and sat with U.N. Dhebar, All India Congress President with the same spirit. He could perform multifarious jobs besides being a top leader at the State level. Once in 1959, he trained 1200 volunteers from tea gardens composed of young boys and girls and conducted a guard of honour to V.K. Krishna Menon, the Defence Minister of India, on the occasion of inauguration of the Annual Conference of the Indian National Trade Union Congress (I.N.T.U.C.) held at Dibrugarh. The volunteers were in uniforms with Gandhi caps and Dalbirsingh Lohar himself commanded the guard of honour as the Chief of the Volunteers.

As a social worker Dalbirsingh was always alive to the miseries, death and destruction suffered by people during natural calamities. After the great earthquake of 1950 the river Brahmaputra flooded every year and caused untold miseries to the people of Assam. Dalbirsingh Lohar, in his capacity as an M.L.A. not only helped them with relief measures but also forcefully pleaded in the Assam Assembly to provide timely and adequate relief and rehabilitation to the flood victims. He also urged the Government to take necessary measures to prevent recurrence of floods.

During the Chinese aggression in 1962, the Chinese troops

advanced up to Bomdilla of NEFA. For fear of further advance of the Chinese Tezpur town was deserted and the People of the town were evacuated by the Government. Many European tea garden Managers fled their gardens and the garden workers including the people in general were seized by great panic. At this juncture Dalbirsingh Lohar personally visited many tea gardens, met the tea garden workers and advised them not to panic, but to take courage and stay on.

While looking after the welfare of the people in general, he did not lose sight of the rights and privileges of the Nepalis living in Assam. Many a time he raised point of order in the floor of the Assembly and demanded justice to the Gorkhas who are denied their social and political rights. On 18th/19th July, 1946 he placed the following question before the Assembly :

Question No. 3 – Will the Government be pleased to state :

(a) The present number of Nepalese now residing in Assam.

(b) The number of Nepalese who have permanently settled in Assam.

(c) In what section of the population the Nepalese were included in the last census ?

(d) Whether those Nepalese who have permanently made Assam their home enjoy the same privileges and rights with other settlers with regard to (1) Settlement of land (2) franchise, and (3) election.

The above questions which deal with vitally important aspects of the rights and privileges of the Gorkhas and are normally denied to them in Assam indicate how Dalbirsingh Lohar intended to help the Gorkhas of Assam.

All good things have their ends, as also all noble men have to depart from this world. Shramik Neta Dalbirsingh Lohar's end of life came on the 29th July, 1969 at his residence at Khalihamari, Dibrugarh.

Appendix - I

The Gorkha Recipients of INA Gallantry Medals

1.	Krishna Bahadur Sonar	-	SATRUNASH MEDAL
2.	Purna Bahadur Rai	-	- do –
3.	Capt. Surya Bahadur	-	VEER-E-HIND MEDAL
4.	Capt. Dilman Rai	-	- do –
5.	Capt. Man Bahadur	-	SADAR-E-HIND
6.	Capt. Dilman Singh	-	- do –
7.	Maj. Purna Singh Khawas	-	- do –
8.	Capt. Dal Bahadur Thapa	-	- do –
9.	Capt. Dil Bahadur Rai	-	- do –
10.	Lt. Durga Bahadur	-	SANAD-E-BAHADURI

Appendix - II

Names of the Gorkha Martyrs who joined the INA and laid down their lives for liberation of India

1.	Major Durgamalla Thapa	Hanged to death in Delhi jail on 25th August, 1944
2.	Capt. Dal Bahadur Thapa	Joined INA in 1942, sentenced to death on 3rd May, 1945, in Delhi Jail
3.	Lance Naik Bahadur Singh	Soldier in 2/9 GR. Joined INA as L/Naik and killed in action at Pyinmana, Burma
4.	Naik Man Bahadur Thapa	Joined INA in Singapore in 1942. Served in the Ist Bahadur Group and killed in action.
5.	L/Naik Damar Bahadur	Joined INA in 1942 and killed in action.
6.	Kul Bahadur	Joined INA in Burma in the Body Guard Battalion and died in Burma.
7.	Gyan Bahadur Lama	Joined INA in Malaya as L/Naik. Killed in Action in Burma, on 11 February, 1945.
8.	Man Singh	Soldier in 2/1 GR. Joined INA in 1942 as Havildar in Bahadur Group and got killed.
9.	Mohan Singh Gorkha	Soldier in 2/1 GR. Joined INA in Malaya as Havildar. Killed in action in July 1944.

10. Prem Bahadur	L/Naik in Indian Army, Medical Corps. Joined INA in Malaya, died in Burma in July 1944.
11. Sital Bahadur	A soldier in GR. Joined INA in Malaya. Served as Havildar in Ist Bahadur Group. Killed in Burma in August 1944.
12. Capt. Bhimsingh Thapa	Joined INA in Malaya in 1943. Served as Captain and killed in action.
13. Hav. Mohansingh Thapa	Havildar Clerk in 2/1 GR. Joined INA in Malaya, Served as S.O. in the Ist Bahadur Group. Killed in action.
14. Ram Bahadur Thapa	Joined INA in Malaya. Killed in action near Chindwin river in Burma in February, 1944
15. Jamadar Bhimsen Thapa	Soldier of 3/1 GR Joined INA in 1942 in Ist Bahadur Group and killed in action.
16. Capt. Sher Bahadur Bhandari	2/1 GR. Joined INA in Malaya as Captain in Ist Bahadur Group. Died in hospital in Burma in 1944.
17. Bhowan Singh	Havildar Clerk in 2/9 GR Joined INA in 1942 and killed in action in Burma.
18. L/Naik Bhim Singh	From 2/1 Gr. Joined INA in 1942 as 2nd Lieutenant. Died in action in Burma.
19. Bhupal Singh Gorkha	From 2/5 GR. Joined INA in 1942 as Intelligence Officer. Shot and killed by Enemy on being detected.
20. Hav. Dhan Bahadur	From 1/3 GR. Joined INA in 1942. Killed in action.
21. Dhan Bahadur Gurung	From 2/2 Garhwal Rifles. Joined

	INA as Naik. Killed in action.
22. Manilal Gurung	Havildar Clerk in 2/1 GR. Joined INA in Malaya. Served as S.O. in Ist Bahadur Group. Killed in Burma.
23. Kalu Gorkha	Joined INA in Malaya in Ist Bahadur Group. Died by drowning in 1943.
24. Kalusingh Lama	Joined INA in Malaya. Served as S.O. in Training Centre. Killed in action near Chindwin river in 1943.
25. Dhyan Bahadur	From 2/5 GR. Joined INA in 1942 as Havildar in Ist Bahadur Group. Killed during action in Burma.

Source: Dr. P.N. Chopra – *Who is Who of Indian Martyrs,* Vol. 1, 1969.

Appendix - III

Indo-Nepal Treaty of Peace and Friendship, 1950

The Government of India and the Government of Nepal, recognising the ancient ties which have happily existed between the two countries for centuries, desiring still further to strengthen and develop these ties and to perpetuate peace between the two countries, have resolved, therefore, to enter into a treaty of peace and friendship with each other, and have, for this purpose, appointed as their plenipotentiaries the following persons, namely,

The Government of India: His Excellency Shri Chandreswar Prasad Narain Singh, Ambassador of India in Nepal.

The Government of Nepal: Mohun Shamsher Jang Bahadur Rana, Maharaja, Prime Minister and Supreme Commander-in-Chief of Nepal, who have examined each other's credentials and found them good and in due form have agreed as follows:

ARTICLE – 1

There shall be everlasting peace and friendship between the Government of India and the Government of Nepal. The two governments agree mutually to acknowledge and respect the complete sovereignty, territorial integrity and independence of each other.

ARTICLE – 2

The two governments hereby undertake to inform each other of any serious friction or misunderstanding with any neighbouring state likely to cause any breach in the friendly relations subsisting between the two governments.

ARTICLE – 3

In order to establish and maintain the relations referred to in Article 1 the two governments agree to continue diplomatic relations with each other by means of representative with such staff as is necessary for the due performance of their functions.

The representatives and such of their staff as may be agreed upon shall enjoy such diplomatic privileges and immunities as are customarily granted by international law on a reciprocal basis, provided that in no case shall, these be less than those granted to persons of similar status of any other State having diplomatic relations with either governments.

ARTICLE -4

The two governments agree to appoint consuls-general, vice-consuls and other consular agents, who shall reside in towns, ports and other places in each other's territory as may be agreed to.

Consuls-general, consuls, vice-consuls and consular agents shall be provided with exequaturs or other valid authorization of their appointment, liable to be withdrawn by the country which issued it, if considered necessary. The reasons for the withdrawal shall be indicated wherever possible.

The persons mentioned above shall enjoy on a reciprocal basis all the rights, privileges, exceptions and immunities that are accorded to persons of corresponding status of any other State.

ARTICLE- 5

The Government of Nepal; shall be free to import from or through the territory of India, arms, ammunitions or warlike material and equipment necessary for the security of Nepal. The procedure for giving effect to this arrangement shall be worked out by the two governments acting in consultation.

ARTICLE – 6

Each government undertakes, in token of the neighbourly friendship between India and Nepal, to give to the nationals of the other, in its territory, national treatment with regard to participation in industrial and economic development of such territory and to the grant of concessions and contracts relating to such development.

ARTICLE -7

The Government of India and Nepal agree to grant, on a reciprocal basis, to the nationals of one country in the territories of the other the same privileges in the matter of residence, ownership of property, participation in trade and commerce, movement and other privileges of a similar nature.

ARTICLE -8

So far as matters dealt with herein are concerned, this treaty cancels all previous treaties, agreements and engagements entered into on behalf of India between the British Government and the Government of Nepal.

ARTICLE- 9

This treaty shall come into force from the date of signature by both governments.

ARTICLE -10

This treaty shall remain in force until it is terminated by either party by giving one year notice.

Done in duplicate at Kathmandu this 31st day of July, 1950.

(Sd) Chandreswar Prasad Narain Singh
For the Government of India
(Sd) Mohan Shamsher Jang Bahadur Rana
For the Government of Nepal.

Appendix-IV

Externment Order of the Governor of Assam Served on Bhakta Bahadur Pradhan

Government Notification

Order No. 13168-H dated Shillong the 8th December, 1941

Whereas the Governor is satisfied with respect to the under mentioned person that with a view to preventing him from acting in a manner prejudicial to the defence of Brities India and the maintenance of public order, it is necessary to make the following order.

Now, therefore, in exercise of the power conferred by sub-rule (1) clause (c) of Rule 26 of the Defence of India Rules, the Governor is plased to direct that the said undermentioned person shall not, after the expiry of a period of 72 hours from the receipt of this order, be in any place within the districts of Lakhimpur, Sibsagar, Darrang, Nowgong and Kamrup, being districts within the province of Assam.

Bhakta Bahadur Pradhan, son of Jit Bahadur of Digboi, Lakhimpur district and of Bokelgoan, Police Station Dibrugarh, Lakhimpur district.

Sd.

The Chief Secretary

Government of Assam

Copy to Officer-in-Charge,

Dibrugarh P.S. for service and return

the duplicate copy to be duly received

by the externee concerned.

Appendix-V

Dibrugrh District Congress Committee
Certificate of Political Sufferer

Congress Bhawan
Dibrugarh

Ref. No.........

This is certiry that Shri (ns) Bhakta Bahadur Pradhan son of Shri Jit Bahadur Pradhan of Digboi is a Political Sufferer of the Sub-Division. He lost his service of Assam Oil Co. Ltd. Digboi, suffered imprisonment for one year and he was externed from Assam by the then British Government for joining the political movement of India's Independence during 1939-42.

As such, he falls under the category I as per difinition of Political sufferers.

He deserves consideration from Government as Political Sufferer.

S/d Indreswar Khound
President, District
Congress Committee
Dibrugarh.

Bibliography

Chopra, P.N – *Who is Who of Martyrs*, Vol. I, 1967.

Gordon, Leonard, A – *Brothers Against Raj*, New Delhi, 1990.

Giani, K.S, - *Indian Independence Movement in East Asia*, 1947.

Harclerode, Peter and Reynold David–*Gurkhas*, 2003, London.

Hussain, M – *The Assam Movement*, 1993, Nanak Publication, Delhi.

Hussain, Imdad – *Soldiers and Settlers: The Recruitment of Gorkhas in North* East India, Ed.A.C.Sinha and T.B. Subba, The *Nepalis in The North East India.*

Khan, Shah Nawaz, *My Memories of INA and its Netaji.*

Lebra, Joice C – *Jungle Alliance : Japan and India National Army.*

Muktan, K.K – *The Legendary Gorkhas*, 2002, Spetrum Publication, Guwahati.

Report of the Land and Revenue Administration of Assam, 1919-20.

Report of the Land and Revenue Administration of Assam Valley Div., 1939-40.

Sarma, L.P., *Indian National Movement.*

Singh, S.K., *Tribal Mevement in India.*

Sinha, A.C. The Indian North East Frontier and Nepalis Immigration in *Himalayan Environment and Culture*, (ed.) N.K. Rustamji and Charles Ramble, New Delhi, 1990.

Shakespear, Col. L.W, *History of Assam Rifles*, 1929.

Upadhyaya, B.L., *Asame Nepaliharu* (in Nepali), Tezpur, 1984.

———— *Khan Mihali* (Assamese), 2004.

————*Karmabir Chhabilal Upadhyaya*,(in Nepali), 1985.

————*Swadhinata Sangrami Shramik Neta, Dalbir Singh Lohar* (in Assamese).

———— *Bhakta Bahadur Pradhan, 1990* (in Nepali).

Dr. Khemraj, *Bishnulal Upadhyaya, Byaktitwa ra Krititwa, 2004* (in Nepali).

Newspapers

Amrit Bazar Patrika, dated 1st April, 1980.

Assam Tribune, dated 1st May, 1980.

Bulletin, Assam Gorkha Sammelon (1-3-69 to 1981).

Bhakta Bahadur Pradhan (Freedom Fighter)

Bishnulal Upadhyaya (Freedom fighter)

Dalbir Singh Lohar (Freedom Fighter)

Dr Manmohan Singh, Prime Minister, pressing the button to unveil the statue of Durga Malla

Gorkha Marching Band

Gorkha Rifles Contingent

Netaji Subhas Chandra Bose

Shaheed Durga Malla

Shaheed Durga Malla's statue in Hamiltongunj in Delhi

Sharda Malla wife of Shaheed Durga Malla

Index